Diamond Bricks Live On
in the
Scandinavian Village

by
EDGAR WALZ

ISBN 1-57579-113-7

Printed in United States of America

PINE HILL PRESS, INC.
Freeman, S. Dak. 57029

ii

Concordia Senior College becomes the historical bridge leading LC—MS Ministerial Education from a German heritage to an international outreach.

Table of Contents

Foreword

Dr. Edgar Walz has written a superlative account of a very special institution in a manner that describes the human as well as the formal characteristics. Concordia Senior College was marked by a vision and excellence in the liberal arts at a level rare in higher education.

Inaugurated in a period of competitive and rigorous academic endeavor in American culture as a whole, the administration and faculty brought expertise and consecration to the task of preparing theological students for seminary education.

Few students who experienced the nurture of Concordia Senior College can forget its excellence and impact on their formation.

Enjoy Dr. Walz's tour of the planning, the people and the campus that made the institution so extraordinary.

Dr. Dean Wenthe, President
Concordia Theological Seminary
(An alumnus of Concordia Senior College)

Preface

This book is about change in the Lutheran Church—Missouri Synod. It deals specifically with the way we have changed our system for training pastors. For more than 150 years the Lord has been with us as we took care of this important part of our church's ministry. And for more than 84 of those 150 years God has given me the personal privilege of being connected with this ministry.

It started at Trinity Lutheran Church in Heilbronn (Freeman, S. Dak.). This little country church was the first Missouri Synod Church in the Dakota Territory. Here I was baptized by Pastor Doege on May 3, 1914. Here I learned about my Savior, Jesus. Here I went to parochial school. Here I was confirmed. Here's where I decided to to go to Concordia St. Paul, Minn. and Concordia Seminary St. Louis to become a pastor in the LC-MS. Here I was married.

During my prep school years at St. Paul I developed a desire, some day, to become a professor at one of Synod's ministerial colleges. Professor Blankenbuehler at St. Paul encouraged me to pursue that goal but also advised me to get five to ten years experience as a parish pastor. I followed that advice when I served parishes at Norris, Lebanon, and Mitchell, S. Dak.

At Lebanon, just four years after I had graduated from the seminary, I enrolled for an additional year toward the B. A. which had been added after I graduated. I took college courses at Northern State Teachers College, Dakota Wesleyan University, and the University of South Dakota and sent the credits to Concordia St. Louis. In 1946 I received my B. A.

During the same year, I accepted a call to teach at Concordia Lutheran High School, operating on the campus of Concordia College, Fort Wayne, IN. For the next forty seven years I served the synodical ministerial education system as a faculty and administrator. I was directly involved with the sale of Concordia Junior College, Fort Wayne, IN,with the construction, operation and closing of Concordia Senior College, with a year of joint occupancy of the Fort Wayne Saarinen campus, and as an adjunct professor of Concordia Theological Seminary until my retirement in 1993. Since my retirement I've still kept in close contact with the faculty and staff of the seminary.

This book, written at the invitation of Seminary President Dean Wenthe, is an attempt to share my personal involvement with LC-MS's ministerial education. What I share includes personal observations and opinions. Obviously, my personal biases affect what I write. May these words help the reader to appreciate God's guidance in training pastors for the Lutheran Church—Missouri Synod.

Abbreviations

BHE	Board for Higher Education of the LC—MS
CSC	Concordia Senior College, Fort Wayne, IN
CTS	Concordia Theological Seminary, Fort Wayne, IN
EW	Dr. Edgar Walz
FT. W	Concordia College, the four year high school plus two year college program, modeled after the German "Gymnasium."
HGB	Dr. Herbert G. Bredemeier
LC—MS	Lutheran Church—Missouri Synod
MJN	Dr. Martin J. Neeb
PERRY COUNTY	Lutheran Saxon Immigrants who settled in Perry County, Missouri in 1839.
SCANDINAVIAN	1953-1977: Concordia Senior College, Fort Wayne, IN. VILLAGE After 1977: Concordia Theological Seminary, Fort Wayne, IN.
SPRINGFIELD	Practical Seminary established by Wyneken/Siehler/Loehe in Fort Wayne, IN in 1848, later moved to Concordia Seminary, St. Louis and operated as a separate practical seminary along side of the Theoretical program. Later moved to Springfield, IL and in 1976 to Fort Wayne, IN.
ST. L	Theoretical Seminary moved from Perry County to St. Louis. Generally referred to as THE seminary.
WW I	World War I
WW II	World War II

Introduction

A Scandinavian Village in Fort Wayne, Indiana? In Norway, or Sweden or Finland perhaps, but not in Indiana. Or even in Wisconsin, or Minnesota or one of the Dakotas, but not in a German community like Fort Wayne. Yet there it stands, hidden behind the trees, like a little town in Finland.

What's it doing here? How did it get here? What goes on here?

It was put here, more than forty years ago, by the Lutheran Church—Missouri Synod. They have their headquarters in St. Louis, Missouri. They actually started in Perry County, Missouri, about a hundred miles south of St. Louis. And for the first hundred years of their existence, they were as German as any church could be. In fact, their major mission from the very beginning was to find the scattered German Lutheran immigrants, who were settling in rural mid-western America.

The following pages will take you through the "seemingly misplaced" Scandinavian Village. They will explain the the village layout. You will read about the diamond shaped "Concordia" bricks and the way that they were used to bring life into a campus for preministerial students who upon their graduation would proceed to Concordia Seminary in St. Louis to become pastors of the Lutheran Church—Missouri Synod.

The book takes you back to the very beginning of the LC-MS's way of educating pastors. It points out the importance which the Synod placed upon a system of ministerial training. The system was patterned after the German "gymnasium," including four years of high school and two years of college. The seminary at St. Louis accepted only the "Prep" school graduate; the seminary in Springfield took students from whatever level of education they came and supplied high school and college as it deemed necessary before the study of theology.

The chapters also trace the changes which were brought to the system as time went on and as the membership of the LC-MS included more and more second and third generation American born German members. After World War I the desire for four years of college before entering the St. Louis seminary became more and more vocal. The resistance emphasized the importance of the strong classical and language emphasis which existed through the years. The resistance ignored or at least minimized the importance of adding natural science and social science college courses.

During the 1930's the demand for change became so strong that Synod introduced a minor change by adding a college year to the St. Louis seminary program, granting an "unaccredited" B. A. after the second year at the seminary. This change, however, did not really satisfy the desire of seminary graduates and certainly not the entrance requirements for graduate study in most American colleges and universities.

Finally, Dr. Martin J. Neeb, Executive Secretary of Synod's Board for Higher Education, with powerful research made on Synod's long standing "prep" school system, and with strong support from "prep" school faculties and also of a growing number of parish pastors succeeded in getting the 1947 Centennial synodical convention in Chicago to pass a resolution to establish a college bachelor's degree as an entrance requirement for the study of theology at the St. Louis seminary.

Dr. Neeb's preparation of the curriculum was just as careful and thorough as his preliminary research had been. His recommendation for a two-year upper level separate senior college with the retention of the traditional "prep' school system was a careful effort to retain the treasured system of the past as well as to include what had been missing from the B. A. degree granted by the St. Louis seminary.

The location in Fort Wayne was a compromise in an effort to increase the approved cost budget by a million dollars. The selection of a well known architect brought him to Eero Saarinen, who happened to have been born in Finland, and who came up with a recommendation of a Scandinavian Village to be erected on the former Kramer farm. It took ten years between the centennial Chicago convention resolution to change and the enrollment of the first students at Concordia Senior College.

The short twenty year performance of Concordia Senior College is really the central topic of this book. In spite of preliminary doubt and resistance, the senior college program took off with a "bang." Glowing reports in secular architectural and educational journals, as well as, an endless series of progress reports in the "Lutheran Witness" and other Lutheran journals, temporarily and on the surface, at least, overpowered and silenced all opposition.

To be a part of the excitement of almost two hundred students coming from the the hundred-year prep school system of LC-MS ministerial training and stepping into a new and untried environment of Concordia Senior College in the Scandinavian Village of Fort Wayne, Indiana was truly "an historic occasion." The faculty was as ready for this new educational venture as any faculty could be. Students and faculty moved forward with an enthusiasm that had no parallel in recent liberal arts education.

Classroom achievement was outstanding. Student cooperation was exceptional. The whole atmosphere in the Scandinavian Village was truly inspiring. Before you knew it, the first year was ended. And everyone was busy preparing for the following September. A whole new set of courses awaited the returning seniors. For the incoming new junior class improvements stimulated by the previous year's experience were challenging. Performance of seniors on national graduate record exams proved that they could hold their own among American colleges in psychology, philosophy, literature and history.

In addition to producing graduates that were truly prepared for the study of theology at the St. Louis Seminary, faculty and administration were also feverishly preparing for accreditation by North Central. Under the guidance of a special consultant they put in hours and days getting ready for the visitation of accreditation examiners. Students and faculty were ready to rejoice over the enthusiastic report which the north central team shared with the Senior College community. Full accreditation of an upper level liberal arts program was the answer. The skeptics who had questioned the possibility were silenced.

Enrollments kept growing. The church's predicted need for future pastors was most encouraging. Before a decade was past space limits at CSC had been reached. With understandable hesitancy the administration accepted the synodical decision to add a second classroom building and to erect dormitories for another hundred students.

But times kept changing. Students in the late 1960's were no longer willing to be regimented through a system of ministerial training as they had been a decade before. And the junior colleges were no longer content remaining less than full four-year degree granting institutions. Eventually competition and opposition in the church at large as well as rumblings of discontent within CSC brought about a decline from the heights of the Senior College's achievement and popularity. The times and attitudes would no longer accept the unique "prep" school, senior college, seminary route for ministerial training in LC-MS.

In addition, Synod's 1969 move to what some called a political party system of leadership affected the church's educational institutions. Eventually, the 1975 convention in Anaheim voted to close Concordia Senior College and to have the Springfield seminary take over the Scandinavian Village in Fort Wayne. On July 1, 1977 Concordia Theological Seminary became the legal successor to Concordia Senior College.

The last two chapters of the book briefly summarize some changes brought about by the closing of the Senior College and the return of the Springfield seminary to the city where it began 130 years before. It was hard for the senior college faculty and staff to adjust to the change. And it was difficult for the Springfield faculty to leave their homes and come to Fort Wayne. The general public had troubles understanding what had happened.

Chapter twelve deals with campus changes which were made to buildings and grounds. It also points out the people differences which a seminary brought. Over time the community too, adjusted to the differences.

Chapter thirteen deals with the seminary campus purpose and campus activities. It emphasizes the central purpose for which the Scandinavian Village was originally established. Though the basic activity is different, it is, nevertheless, still a school owned and operated by the Lutheran Church-Missouri and used to prepare men for ministry. The scope is worldwide. The emphasis is on missions. Graduates go all over the world to bring the Gospel of Jesus Christ to people everywhere.

CHAPTER I

A Scandinavian Village in Fort Wayne

A. ENTRANCE

Entrance signs to the Concordia campus have changed over the years. During the intitial construction which in 1954 began to convert the Kramer farm to an upper level preministerial college, a temporary sign did the job.

1954

When the first students came to enroll in 1957 a permanent sign identified the new Senior College.

Main Campus Entrance soon after "The Beginning."

When the Springfield seminary moved in to operate with the Senior College during its last year in 1976, a temporary combination of signs greeted the campus visitor.

1976

Since July 1, 1977, when Concordia Theological Seminary took possession of the campus, the Scandinavian Village in Fort Wayne has been the place from which pastors have been sent to congregations and missions all over the world.

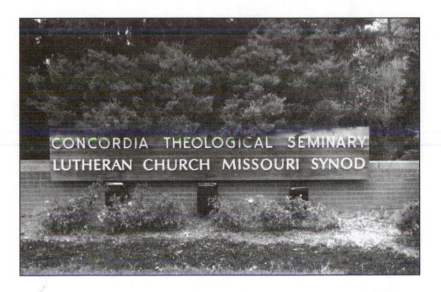

That begins the story of the Scandinavian Village in Fort Wayne, Indiana.

B. BUILDING LOCATIONS: (1957)

Just follow the winding road through the woods and up the hill and stop. Take a good look at what's ahead of you and then move on. If you'd turn right on Coverdale Drive you'd see a group of wooden faculty homes and a large brick president's house by itself at the end of the street. For now follow Martin Luther Drive about a quarter mile east to the curve which leads you left. There's a group of strangely shaped brick buildings clustered together. As you slowly drive toward them you forget the busy world from which you came. You're coming to the center of The Scandinavian Village in Fort Wayne, Indiana.

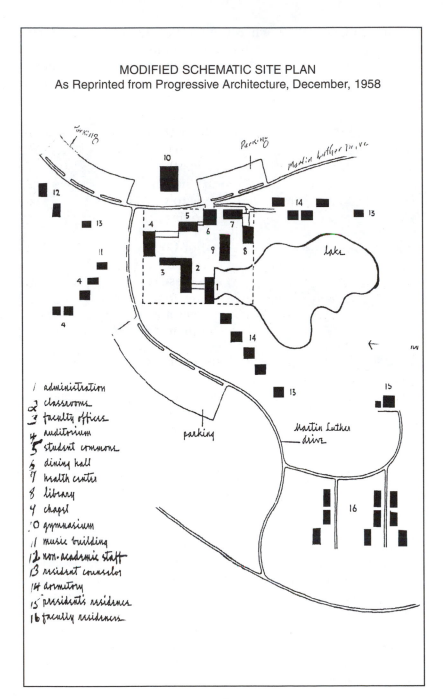

MODIFIED SCHEMATIC SITE PLAN
As Reprinted from Progressive Architecture, December, 1958

1 administration
2 classrooms
3 faculty offices
4 auditorium
5 student commons
6 dining hall
7 health center
8 library
9 chapel
10 gymnasium
11 music building
12 non-academic staff
13 resident counselor
14 dormitory
15 president's residence
16 faculty residences

parking

parking

Martin Luther Drive

Martin Luther drive

lake

4

1. Village Central Circle

Look at the site plan on the previous page to get an idea of the "village" arrangement. That's the way business buildings were grouped in the village in Finland where Eero Saarinen, the campus architect, spent his childhood. He arranged the active work buildings of what was to become the campus of Concordia Senior College just like he remembered people were doing things in his childhood. And so he suggests that the roots of the new college extend back over several generations.Here, too, people will come to the center of the village to work during the day and then go back home in the evening to be with their families.

The students, faculty and staff of Concordia Senior College would do their work in an inner circle of related buildings away from the places where they lived. In these central buildings learning and teaching, relaxation and play, food preparation and dining, library study and research, prayer and worship could all be connected as everyone went about their daily work activities.

The almost vertical lines of the enormous chapel roof on the highest elevation of the circle direct your eyes and mind toward heaven. No one can escape that reminder. That's the message the chapel designer gives to students, teachers, administrators, staff, and visitors day after day. God is always central in our lives and activity.

Young men, graduated from pre-ministerial junior colleges, came here to broaden their understanding of God's universe, to mature in their personal lives as faithful men of God, to develop their communication skills prior to their enrollment at Concordia Seminary in St. Louis. Their entire pre-seminary education was designed to help them know something about everything and everything about something. Their life's purpose was to be effective proclaimers of God's priority in the universe, and especially of His Savior love in Christ Jesus who died on Calvary's cross and victoriously arose from the dead. Earth is our place for useful activity here and now, but our ultimate goal is to be with God in heaven forever. That's the central message of Saarinen's design of this campus.

2. Student Dormitories

The site plan shows three groups of buildings (# 14) branching away from the central circle. Each of these three branches is a group of small, homelike, student dormitories. Each dorm had seventeen double student rooms. In addition, each dorm also provided a special study room which could be used by individuals or small groups, a large lounge with fireplace, like a family living room for larger gatherings, and a small prayer chapel. The student rooms were located on four different floor levels. This avoided the long hallways one usually finds in college dorms. In this homelike atmosphere students could develop good personal relations with their peers.

3. Resident Counselors

A family home (# 13) was a part of each dormitory group. Here lived the resident faculty counselor with his family. This enabled individuals and small groups of dormitory students to spend time away from their "dorm home" and be with a faculty member in the home with his family. This gave the counselor somewhat of a role as an older brother or even a parent.

4. Recreation Facilities

The gymnasium (#10) and the athletic fields were located across the street from the working buildings of the central circle. Here intramural sports were provided for students as well as for faculty families and their friends. Concordia's athletic facilities concentrated more on personal physical development than on competitive sports.

5. On-campus Faculty Homes

At some distance from the central village, near the campus front entrance is a group of faculty homes provided to faculty families instead of a cash housing allowance. These one-story three-bedroom homes, styled almost identically, were all painted the same gray color. Each home provided the professor with a home study/office near the back entrance. Here students, if they chose, could request meetings with the professor without disturbing the professor's family in the rest of the home.

6. President's Home

The home provided for the president and his family was located at some distance from the faculty home group as well as from the central activity and student dormitory groups. This gave the president's home a certain special identity while at the same time providing him with proximity and easy access to everything that happened on campus.

C. ROOF LINES:

Roof lines as seen from campus entrance

The roof lines, as you view them from the distance, are an important unifying factor of the campus. The angles of the roofs are identical to those of diamond bricks arranged horizontally. These half-diamond-shaped lines on roofs, on dominant building walls, as well as the decorative glazed lattices at various inner campus locations all emphasize that the activities within the walls are this-worldly.

Quite in contrast are the roof line of the chapel. These, with the same diamond brick shape rest vertically on the ground and keep pointing upward toward heaven. One cannot escape this horizontal and vertical contrast. Student dormitory or gymnasium, classroom building or faculty home, everything on the whole campus is tied together with activity on this earth. And yet, everything is drawn together by the dominant chapel and pointed upward so that we may always remember that we need to serve God in everything we do.

After that general description its time to take a closer look.

Chapter 2

A Campus Tour Illustrates the Meaning and Purpose of the Scandinavian Village (1957)

A. Central Circle Buildings

1. Classroom Building.

a. Speech Department

The rooms straight ahead and to the left as we enter the classroom building were originally built as the Concordia Senior College speech department. This was at the time when audiotapes were just beginning to find common use in education.

Public speaking was considered an important preparation for the student before he entered the seminary. The Senior College Speech instruction took place in a central classroom for about 30 students surrounded by a number of smaller practice rooms and places for private or semi-private attention.

Hallway—Classroom Building

9

b. Architectural Contrast

The first floor hallway of the classroom building gives us an interesting Saarinen design experience. Floor to ceiling windows overlook the lake and the campus beyond. Diamond shaped glass sections, built with diamond bricks laid on their sides, emphasizes the "this-worldy" nature of the activities which take place here. This is in sharp contrast to the "heaven-pointing" activity which occurs in the chapel so clearly visible through the huge picture windows.

c. Founder's Plaque

As we turn left to walk up the "free-hanging" stairs to the second floor we can't miss a metal wall-plaque listing the names and positions of the officers involved with the activity of producing the Concordia Senior College Campus.

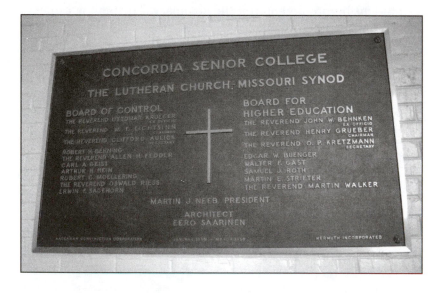

Proceeding up the stairs to the second floor, we turn to

d. The Science Lecture Hall

Required science courses for the pre-seminary students were limited to professorial lectures and demonstrations. Laboratory space was added later.

The front wall of the science lecture room again emphasizes diamond bricks laid horizontally. Thus, as students and faculty as well as visitors move from room to room, they cannot miss the silent message of campus activities for this world, contrasted with the ultimate purpose of study and life to serve the Lord who rules heaven and earth.

e. Split level classrooms

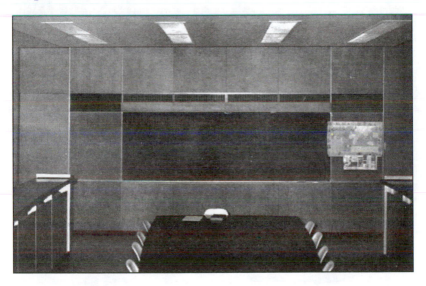

Two level class rooms provided an atmosphere for professor and students to face and freely interact with each other. The chalkboard and projection screen could easily be seen by every student from his position around the large table. Student seating was provided with comfortable contoured plastic chairs. (When students later were asked for the room design preferences when a second class room was planned and designed, the choice was strongly for the split level room.)

The classroom design and furniture provides for teacher learner interaction and for discussion methods of teaching over the lecture/note-taking/recitation methods of former generations. This, in turn, emphasized listening, hearing, thinking, and reacting over against an older method of receiving, remembering, and recalling.

f. Major Campus Mosaic

As we move beyond the second floor hall way we step into a ceiling-high- passage-way to the faculty office building. Here, a major mosaic art piece decorates the entire west wall. This literally dominates the entire campus. The huge mosaic can be lighted by the bright eastern sun or by powerful floodlights focusing on it at night.

2. Faculty Office Building

Full time faculty members had small private offices on the main floor of the faculty office building. During the school year two full-time secretaries provided help to all of the faculty members located here. This was also the place where mail was distributed to faculty members and their families. The president did not believe that rural mail boxes should be located in the faculty home area. Thus they and their families depended upon mail distribution through the student mail room on campus with this set of mail boxes in the faculty office building. Faculty members whose offices were in the library or administration building had their mail delivered to the respective secretaries' office.

A faculty lounge was located near the faculty secretaries' office. Here the faculty and administrators routinely gathered each morning after chapel for snacks and coffee and for opportunities to meet with each other on a one to one basis.

Originally, the basement of the faculty office building was an unfinished store room. This space was locked and under the management of administrative and maintenance personnel.

3. Auditorium

The auditorium is intended for large group gatherings. It is rarely used for day to day campus activities.

The building provides comfortable theater seats installed on a steeply inclined floor and facing a curtained stage. A theatrical lighting system provided stage footlights, floodlights, and spotlights.

During the 1957 school year, while the Kramer chapel was still under construction, the auditorium was the place for daily morning and evening campus chapel services.

During the long winter months Friday night movies were shown to campus residents and to faculty families plus any other guests whom students and faculty brought in.

Once a year the faculty, under Paul Harms, would present local humorous dramas, written by faculty and acted by members of the faculty. Students looked forward to and remembered these occasions as some of the highlights of their lighter non academic experiences.

4. Student Commons Building

The student commons building provided many kinds of services to students, faculty, staff. There was a lounge with a log-burning fire place. It was furnished with comfortable chairs and couches and a large-screen television. Here one could spend a little time to relax between scheduled activities. Here one came come to play pool. Here was a sub post office. Here was also the campus book store. Downstairs there's a snack bar. For dormitory students the student commons was like the country store to which one could come to buy, to visit, to watch people, or just to get away from the daily grind.

5. Dining Hall

A glass enclosed walk way connects the student commons with the dining hall. As you enter you see diamond bricks, installed horizontally in solid walls or in diamond shaped glazed panels. Stairways lead to a spacious mezzanine. At the east end of the mezzanine there's a glassed-in private dining room. This private dining room has a floor to ceiling east glass wall, providing a view of the gymnasium and the spacious athletic fields to the very edge of the campus property.

The private dining room was used for scheduled dinner meetings of faculty, administrators, and occasionally official campus visitors. The mezzanine provides dining space for unscheduled gatherings of student and/or faculty groups who choose to eat together semi-privately.

The spacious downstairs dining room is the place where most campus students come for their three meals per day. Concordia Senior College graduates fondly remember the special dinners and banquets which they shared here. Occasional parties and receptions of students, their families or of faculty and/or staff and their families, were also held in the dining hall.

6. Health Center

The health center was really a campus hospital. When dorm students became ill, but not seriously enough to be taken to a community hospital, they were removed from their dormitory rooms and cared for in the health center. When the campus first

14

opened, two professor's wives, who were registered nurses, were employed by the college on a part-time basis. The south entrance led to three private bedrooms which were available to official campus guests.

After the seminary took possession of the campus, the patient rooms, guest rooms, and nurses' room walls were removed. The building was converted into a large lounge and furnished with comfortable chairs and couches.

7. The Library

The college library functioned under the capable direction of Professor Lando Otto and his assistant Margaret Hermes. An open stack system gave easy access to research books and periodicals for all required and elective courses.

The card cataloging was meticulously managed by Margaret Hermes. She was known by all for her precision and accuracy. While she supervised the work of clerical assistants and part-time student librarians, she, personally produced the card catalog as books were acquired.

Faculty members gave the librarian requests for books for their courses and for books in which they as faculty were interested for research. When the LC-MS closed Concordia Senior College in 1977 most of its library holdings were transferred to Concordia College in Ann Arbor, Michigan.

Private faculty offices for Dormitory Counselors were located on the top floor of the three story library building. The rationale for this location was to provide privacy for student consultations.

8. The Chapel

The very heart and center of the campus, of course, is the Kramer Memorial Chapel.

Its location on the highest elevation of the campus rolling land emphasizes importance and dominance. All other buildings of the central village quietly direct peoples' eyes heavenward. On this campus it's hard to forget that we are God's people. Here's a quiet country village, away from worldly distractions.

Kramer Chapel—1957

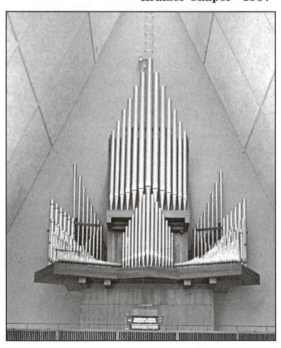

Schlicker Organ

16

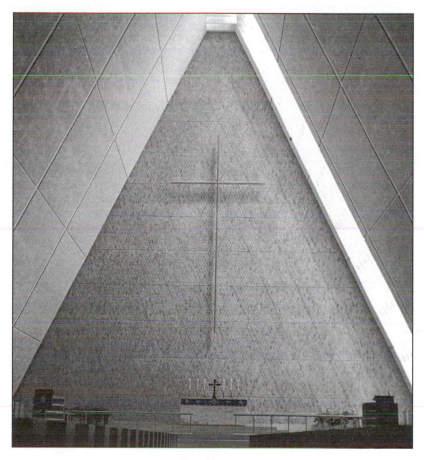

The Chancel

Shaped like a huge diamond brick cut in half and set on end this building stands solid and firm. The adjacent bell tower lifts the Cross to the highest level on campus. The sounding bell invites you to come and worship the Lord. As you enter you stand in silence. The high ceiling draws your eyes to dim light filtering through the tiny skylight. And then the floor to ceiling skylight, which brightens the altar and the majestic aluminum cross on the diamond shaped east wall, beckons you to come forward and be seated. In silence you survey the upward pointing shadows along the length of both walls. You're out of the world, indeed, you're in the very presence of the Lord.

17

The majestic pipes of the Schlicker organ adorn the west diamond brick wall. When the bell stops ringing organ sounds fill the huge space and surround the gathered people. Everyone is drawn to join in songs of praise to the God who meets us here. Students, faculty, and visitors respond in faith to the message which God brings in Word and Sacrament. Reverently they kneel in prayer as they bring their needs in petition and thanks to the Lord. Refreshed and renewed they return to their respective activities of the day.

The chapel, indeed, is the very center of the campus. It lets God lead you forward through a meaningful life.

9. Administration Building

Located nearest to the visitor parking area, with entrance on the lower plaza level and adjacent to the lake, this building provides offices for the president, three deans, the registrar and the business manager. Secretarial staff is provided to each of the administrators.

This is the building handles reception responsibilities for the entire campus. This is the place to which visitors come. Central telephone services are provided through the campus switchboard, operated by the reception secretary. College finances for all departments as well as for student association funds are taken care of by the cashier, the bookkeepers and payment clerks under the supervision of the business manager.

A built-in safe, supervised by the registrar and the business manager, provides security for student academic records, financial records and for cash managed by the business office.

B. Residences
1. Student Dormitories

The Scandinavian Village in Fort Wayne was originally built to provide a relatively self contained quiet place for 450 young men. They came here to acquire a liberal arts bachelor's degree on their way to Concordia Seminary, St. Louis, MO. Their decision to become pastors in the Lutheran Church—Missouri, in most cases, had been made while they attended one of the pre-ministerial junior colleges.

The thirteen dormitories were meant to make a distinctive contribution to each student's two year experience in Fort Wayne. All students were expected to live in the college dorms, to eat their meals in the college dining hall, while they worked their way through the rigorous classical pre-ministerial curriculum. Even students whose families lived within easy driving distance were expected to live on campus.

The dormitory groups give the appearance of large family homes rather than institutional residences. All thirteen dormitories are designed alike. Front entrances lead into a hallway. To the right there's a lounge with fireplace, much like a family living room. A door at the end of the entrance hall leads into the student living area. However, instead of long hall ways on one or two floors, the seventeen individual rooms are placed on four different floor levels. Each room is furnished with beds, desks, and bookshelves for two students. Storage space is available in a large store room on the lowest floor level. Spacious men's restrooms are available on the "fourth" and the basement floors. A snack room with vending machines is on one end of the basement level. A small prayer chapel is available. It provides absolute privacy.

The whole arrangement provides for normal personal development with a group of thirty four men. Here they can study privately along side their room mates, and interact with each other in adjacent rooms. In the large lounge formal business meetings and total group devotions take place. This is also the place where social functions with outside visitors can take place.

2. On Campus Faculty Homes

At some distance from the central village, near the front campus entrance, is a group of faculty homes. Each is provided with a study near its back entrance. Here the professor can do his professorial work at home and also be available at home to the students who choose to consult with him here.

The home provided for the president and his family is located at some distance from the faculty homes, from the central village, and from student dormitories. This gives the president's home a certain special identity while at the same time providing proximity and easy access to everything that goes on.

C. Service Buildings
1. Gymnasium

The gymnasium is located at the east end of the campus adjacent to the ball diamonds, the tennis courts and the all weather track.

Movable bleachers in the gym plus rows of fixed seats on the balcony provide spectator space for up to a thousand people. By placing a portable stage in front of the east wall and setting folding chairs on the canvass covered playing floor a total three thousand people can be accommodated.

The major purpose of the gymnasium was to serve the students. Concordia Senior College provided "a specialized athletic program to complement the training of professional men, wrote Wilbert Stelzer, the athletic director and head coach. "Pee Wee" Stelzer worked together beautifully with "Curly" Haas to provide good intercollegiate teams in basketball, baseball, and tennis.

Most of "Pee Wee's" and "Curly's" time and effort, went into leading and coaching an intramural program. This provided diversion and recreation for up to five hundred dormitory students. Here they helped develop skills and interests which would carry over and be useful to them as pastors. An exceptionally large proportion of students participated in the intramural program. As a result it was easy for a student to write in the "Spire," the first graduation yearbook: "Our lives have been deeply enriched by athletics at Concordia Senior College."

The spacious facilities also made graduating classes creatively ambitious as they planned and arranged elaborate spring banquets. Some of these "literally" took students, their guests, faculty and staff and their spouses, out of this world.

The Central District of the Lutheran Church—Missouri Synod and later the Indiana District rented the campus facilities for conventions.

2. Maintenance Shops and Storage Buildings

Building and grounds tools and equipment have a number of places. The largest and oldest of them is an old three story cattle barn which was part of the old Kramer farm in the woods near North Clinton. This is a place to keep large grounds machines, building materials, including some diamond bricks which could be used to face exterior walls of new buildings that might be erected. Used lumber and rarely used hand tools are also kept there. Trucks and a few tractors were kept in a special storage shed near the tennis courts.

The office for the secretary of the maintenance building and grounds directors, is on the ground level under the dining room. Adjacent to this in the basement under Luther Hall is storage for furniture for various buildings. Cleaning tools and supplies were also kept here. The large workshop is equipped with power woodworking and metal working tools. Power tools for mowing, fertilizing, irrigating, maintaining streets, and removing snow are maintained and stored in the large garage under the dining hall.

Building operation and cleaning services are centrally directed from the maintenance department office.

The campus heating plant is located in the basement of the auditorium. Central air conditioning machinery is located in the basement of the south classroom building near the faculty office building.

All records, files, finances are administered with the secretarial help in the maintenance office, near the loading dock.

CHAPTER 3

Adjusting the Scandinavian Village to Changing Needs

A. Additions and Improvements (1957-1976)

1. Storm Windows in Student Dormitories

The first winter produced a serious temperature problem for students who lived in dormitories. When the temperature got down to twenty the student rooms could no longer be heated. When the same thing occurred in every dorm, it was clear that it was not a heating system problem.

Architect and contractor inspections concluded that in the Fort Wayne area climate it was not practical to operate the dorms without installing storm windows. Small electric heaters for each room only blew fuses but didn't keep the students warm. So, with extra blankets, and with cold students gladly coming to the dining hall, class rooms, or library, we made it through the winter. The following summer all dorms received storm windows.

2. Business Office Remodeling

We also had to find extra dollars to pay for absolutely essential remodeling costs in the business office.

It seems that space planners had little understanding about what happens in a college business office. The switchboard operator and receptionist had to direct everyone who came into the building in the hearing presence of three other workers who tried to handle mail distribution, cashiering, banking, paying bills and payroll, counting money, filing and dozens of other activities. Needless to say, distraction from all directions became a way of life.

We installed a wall to separate the receptionist function from the business office functions.

While this somewhat lessened the immediate problem, efficiency for business functions was not provided until later when two additional rooms were made available for business office personnel.

3. Additional On-campus Faculty Homes

When the second class of students enrolled in 1958 many new faculty positions needed to be filled. Since the administration's decision to provide faculty homes rather than expect incoming faculty to rent or purchase their own, Concordia Senior College built ten additional homes in the faculty housing area.

These were similar to the original Saarinen homes except they had a one car attached garage instead of free standing car ports. (Because of the cold winters in Fort Wayne, the faculty car ports had by now been converted to enclosed garages.)

Later, additional homes were purchased in the Colonial Park and Concordia Garden neighborhoods.

4. On-Campus Incinerating System

Removing trash from student dormitories, food service and campus offices and classrooms became a major task. The college had to decide whether to hire commercial trash services or to have the maintenance department do the job.

But burning paper and other flammables in open fires was not the answer. Ultimately, it was decided to erect an incinerator on the north campus edge near the tennis courts. While this solved some of the problems, there was still considerable accumulation of ashes and items which could not be burned. After a few years the incinerator was discontinued, the facilities were razed. and commercial trash companies were hired.

5. The North Classroom Building

By the early 60's the reputation of Concordia Senior College had been established. Not only had the national academic community recognized Concordia Senior College with North Central accreditation but the Lutheran Church—Missouri Synod also seemed to accept the new senior college as the preferred route into the ministry.

While the original campus had been designed for about 450 students, that capacity had been reached. Space requirements became more intense as time went on. Predictions of larger future pastor needs suggested that more space be made available at the Senior College in Fort Wayne. It was decided that a class room building equal to the size of the original be added.

That decision became an exciting challenge to faculty, students and administration. After some time this radical change was reluctantly accepted by President Neeb.

The Saarinen architectural form was engaged to lead the project. Location and design had to extend rather than interfere with the intimate relationship which the original inner circle buildings had provided. The placement of the "North Classroom" as it became known, where it is, was the answer.

The unused basement space under the original faculty office building became a convenient corridor.

Everyone on campus had a voice in determining the new building's needs. There was a strong preference for the split-level style. People also asked for larger rooms than those in the original classroom building.

A most unusual room style and size resulted from the request of Prof. Paul Harms, a speech professor and drama coach. The design ended in a theater-in-the round arrangement.

The west end of the first floor of the new building included several rooms to be used by the faculty. One was a new faculty lounge with comfortable furniture and a large screen TV. The lounge was connected to a kitchenette. Here faculty members could come daily after the morning chapel for a little relaxation and to contact each other informally.

Next to this faculty lounge was a large faculty meeting room. This was equipped with comfortable folding chairs, with curtained chalk board and projection screen, and wired for the latest audio visual aids. This room was also the place for faculty and their spouses to hold social gatherings.

Student Personnel services up until this time had been scattered. The counselors' offices were on the second floor of the library. The dean of student's office, on the other hand, was located on the second floor of the administration building. The registrar's office was on the first floor of the administration building.

A series of offices on the east end of the second floor of the new classroom building provided space for the dean of students, his secretary, other faculty and staff workers, and eventually for the registrar's office and his secretary's office as well as the office for the financial aid officer.

The new classroom building provided space for relocating the book store and post office.

Book store space was professionally planned. It provided a receiving processing room, a manager's office with adequate desk and filing space, a cashiering counter, and adjustable display shelves to handle text books, theological books and church supplies. The patronage included students, faculty, staff, city congregations and schools and the general public. The Indiana District eventually bought the church supply department and moved it to its own new office building on Barr street.

Another service area that had developed took care of central duplicating and printing and provided central storage for paper and office supplies. This was located in a large room across the hall from the post office and book store.

6. Additional Student Dormitories

Three additional air conditioned dormitories were located south of the gymnasium parking lot. This group was labeled by the students as "promised village."

These dormitories were built according to the specifications and blueprints of the original thirteen. The college purchased the entire remaining inventory of diamond "Concordia" bricks from the manufacturer in Ohio. Experience with the original 13 dorms led to changing the electric power specifications to handle more electric appliances. Each dorm was equipped with its own heating and air conditioning unit.

7. Fourth Resident Counselor Family Home

To provide the same village-counselor relationship as had been done originally called for building a home for the counselor's family next to the new dorms. It was located along Martin Luther drive toward the east campus exit. It was surrounded by screening evergreen trees which gave the place an estate-like appearance.

8. Athletic Field Expansion

A generous donor provided the funds to build an all weather track in the large space beyond the east dormitory group. This was used by campus students and by various Lutheran grade schools.

The original tennis court surfaces had deteriorated over time. They were replaced with professionally designed and specified all weather surfaces. This made them available for better student use and for setting up rentals for extra income when total student enrollments had begun to decline.

B. Removals (1957-1976)

1. The Original Kramer Family Homestead

The original Kramer homestead was located on the south edge of the campus, near the carrion tower. Only a few trees around the yard still stood. The brick home had been neglected for a long time. The roof had caved in and one sidewall had fallen down. It was not practical to restore and retain the old place . Within a year college maintenance had removed the old bricks and closed the family well. Now it is difficult to tell where the original home stood.

2. The George Sweet residence

Not included with the purchase of the Kramer property was a five acre residential area on the extreme northwest corner of the campus. The only building on the five acres was a small frame house in which George Sweet had spent his declining years.

His housekeeping and care of the property left much to be desired. George used to be seen riding his bicycle carrying a two gallon kerosene can to the filling station about two miles south on Clinton Street. He used the fuel to fire a kerosene burning cook stove and to provide fuel for his oil lamp. Over the years he had stored old newspapers in various rooms and corners, leaving only a little space for himself to move around caring for his basic household activities.

When George died the college maintenance department was confronted with the task of removing the house and its contents. With the consent of the city fire department it was decided to light a match to the place and burn it down.

3. The Howard Kramer Residence

Howard Kramer's parents had relocated from the old homestead to a set of farm buildings in the woods facing Clinton street. The old maintenance storage barn which still stands in the woods was a part of that group.

The campus land purchase agreement had allowed Howard to stay in his home as long as he lived. Howard felt very comfortable with the college maintenance staff and spent many hours watching them work. On very special occasions, like when he was invited to share a campus social function in the dining hall, he would proudly come riding in his new Cadillac sedan.

Eventually only the large storage barn, a little tool shed, a garage, and the brick house remained. After Howard died, students had hoped to convert the old home into some kind of a social gathering facilities. Administration, however, foreseeing possible serious problems with such usage made a quick decision to have all buildings except the maintenance storage barn removed. All that remains now is the cross drive on four lane North Clinton Street, which originally led to the driveway into the Kramer farm.

Chapter 4

Historical Roots of the Scandinavian Village

A. Formative Years (1837-1847)

It took one hundred years for LC—MS to change its original way of educating ministers. And yet over those years the world kept on changing as it always does.

1. Perry County

The Saxon immigrants actually began with the log cabin in Perry County. Four German University graduates, named Buenger, Fuerbringer, Brohm and Walther, with their own hands felled the trees, trimmed the logs and built the the one room log cabin school. This was In the village of Dresden, Missouri, down the Mississippi River from the city of St. Louis. These four men were the builders, the owners, the faculty and the administration. And then, of all things, they dared to advertise for students in the German paper of St. Louis more than fifty miles away.

The school opened December 9, 1839 rather than October as the ad in the St. Louis paper had promised. They needed money to buy furniture and equipment. A donation from Otto Walther's congregation in St. Louis made the opening possible. There were eleven pupils, four girls and seven boys, ranging from age 5 1/2 to 15. The subjects included those which the four teachers had been taught in the German "gymnasium." Preparing students to become ministers was not really the original purpose of the school even though the subjects taught would have prepared the graduates for the study of theology at a seminary.

The school was moved from Dresden, Missouri, where C.F.W. Walther also served as pastor, to Altenburg in 1841. The enrollment of girls terminated in May 1843. This was also the year when, under the direction of Loeber, the school took the new direction of training church workers.

2. St. Louis

Trinity church in St. Louis, where Otto Walther was pastor, took a paternal attitude toward the Perry county educational venture. They assisted with financial support and also sent students to Perry Country to study to become church workers. There was no dormitory. Students lived with faculty families and with church member's families in the Altenburg area. The school became a bond of mutual interest between the St. Louis and the Perry County Lutherans. With it began the system of six year prep schools, before pastors began their study of theology at a seminary. The system continued until 1957 when Synod began the Senior College in the Scandinavian Village in Fort Wayne.

3. Fort Wayne

Meanwhile, another group of Lutherans in Fort Wayne, Indiana, under the pastoral leadership of Hoover, established St. Paul's congregation in 1837 The following year, in 1838, Wyneken succeeded Hoover as pastor of St. Paul's. In addition to serving the Fort Wayne Lutherans as pastor, Wyneken also, on horseback, visited many communities in northeast Indiana, southern Michigan and northwest Ohio, looking for German Lutherans who had settled here but who did not have the services of a pastor. He found the situation most disturbing. In so many places there were German Lutherans who had not had any pastoral services for years. They had no group worship, their children were neither baptized nor confirmed. In short, they had been lost to the church. Wyneken tried his best to serve them as often as he could, but found the task so enormous that it was far beyond his ability to take care of their pastoral needs.

He wrote to his friend, Pastor Loehe in Germany telling him about the pitiful situation about uncared for scattered German Lutherans in America and the need for more pastors to come and serve them. In his parsonage in Fort Wayne he began teaching two men who showed an interest in becoming pastors. Loehe in Germany also gathered young men who under him studied to become missionaries to the scattered German Lutherans in America.

Meanwhile, Wyneken under the stress of his work developed a throat problem. In 1841 he decided to return to his native home in Germany to find medical help. While there he made an earnest plea with Lutherans in Germany to help with men and money to train missionaries to come to America. With his "Notruf" he interested many people in Germany who helped. While Wyneken was gone from Fort Wayne Sihler took care of St. Paul's church and of the training of the students who had begun studying for the ministry in Wyneken's parsonage.

On October 24, 1846 Sihler actually opened the "practical" seminary in Fort Wayne. He and Wyneken had been working with individuals who were interested in becoming pastors. Now Loehe, who had begun training men in Germany, sent eleven students to Fort Wayne. Thus, the Fort Wayne Seminary was underway with individuals whom Wyneken and Sihler had been teaching and with eleven students whom Loehe sent. The Seminary at this time actually belonged to Loehe, even though he remained in Germany.

Rather than emphasizing a classical curriculum like Walther and others had done in Perry county and St. Louis, the Fort Wayne Seminary, because of the urgent need to gather the scattered Lutherans who had been neglected for so long took interested students from whatever level they were in education and in the knowledge of the Bible. They moved them along from the educational level with which they came, giving them as thorough as possible a knowledge of the Old and New Testament, and then led them forward to study the four basic branches of theology, namely, Exegetical, Systematic, Historical, and Practical. The program eventually developed into about three years of pre-seminary and three years of seminary training. With this the young men were ready for calls to gather the scattered German Lutherans in Indiana, Ohio and Michigan. Later, as the development of the Midwest continued into Illinois, Wisconsin, on into Iowa, Minnesota, the Dakota's and eventually Montana and Wyoming all the way to the west coast they sent German Lutheran pastors to gather the scattered German Lutherans into congregations.

B. The Lutheran Church—Missouri Synod is Born

Meanwhile Walther had begun publishing "Der Lutheraner" which reached Lutheran pastors and lay members over Missouri, Ohio and Other states. That publication led German Lutheran pastors to gather together and eventually to form a Synod. After numerous meetings involving especially pastors from the St. Louis and Fort Wayne areas, the Synod was started at a meeting in Chicago in 1847.

1. Fort Wayne

After that, on September 8, 1847 Loehe transferred his seminary in Fort Wayne to the newly organized Missouri Synod. The Fort Wayne Seminary was then under the leadership of A. Wolter. When a cholera epidemic in 1849 ended Wolter's life, A. F. Biewand, a pastor from Washington, D. C., upon Wyneken's advice, took Wolter's place.

2. St. Louis

In 1849 the Perry County and St. Louis Lutherans agreed to move the Altenburg college and seminary to St. Louis. In October,1850 the Perry County academy, college, teacher's college and seminary became the property of the Lutheran Church Missouri Synod. It agreed: 1) To train pastors and teachers to serve Lutheran churches, 2) To do this in German, 3) To retain the pre-seminary academy and college with the seminary, and 4) Also to accept non-church work students. A new building for the school was erected on 2 acres of ground purchased for that purpose near Trinity church in south St. Louis . This, through many subsequent changes remained the place for the St. Louis Seminary until it was relocated on the 90 acre Clayton campus in 1926.

For the time being, Synod owned and operated two separate institutions to train pastors, the practical Seminary in Fort Wayne and the "theoretical seminary" and college in St. Louis.

In 1850 C. F. W. Walther, who had moved to become pastor or Trinity in St. Louis, was called to teach at the Seminary which had moved next to his church. Biewand who the year before, had been called to the Fort Wayne seminary was now called to teach at the St. Louis Seminary. The third member of the St. Louis seminary faculty was Goener. Biewand, incidentally had a strong interest in including English in seminary training for American outreach work. After Biewand died in 1858 interest in English, however, diminished.

The St. Louis Seminary and Synod placed strong emphasis on dealing with scattered German Lutherans. It's interesting to speculate how different the history of LC—MS would have become if Biewand's interest in English had found greater acceptance. (Actually this interest was not realized until after World War I in the 1920's)

3. Fort Wayne

Biewand had actually established an English Academy with the seminary in Fort Wayne. Perhaps because of that action he was moved to St. Louis where a greater emphasis on German existed. In 1852 Synod appointed a committee to study the idea of the English academy in Fort Wayne. Subsequent LC—MS history, however, strongly demonstrated the predominant emphasis on work in German.

Ft. Seminary 1857 on Ind. Institute Campus. (Photo by Ed Walz.)

In 1850 F. A. Cramer, who five years earlier had been sent by Loehe to become pastor of the Lutherans in Frankenmuth, Michigan, was called to head up the Fort Wayne Seminary.

In 1857 a new building (which still stands on the Indiana Institute for Technology campus today-see photo) was erected on a few acres of ground which Synod bought in Fort Wayne for the Seminary and academy. A. Strietelmeyer was called to direct the English academy. That same year a teacher education department (which later led to Addison, Ill., and still later River Forest) also opened on the new Fort Wayne campus. Thus synod actually operated three schools here, a seminary, a teacher's college, and an English academy. One can sense the need for English, especially for teachers who dealt with the younger generation of Lutherans in America.

By 1861 Synod decided on its most drastic change in its American system for teaching pastors and teachers. Synod decided to move the six year "gymnasium" to the Fort Wayne seminary campus and to transfer the Fort Wayne seminary to be combined with the St. Louis seminary.

Schick Hall—Concordia College, Fort Wayne, Indiana. (Postcard)

4. St. Louis

So Cramer and his Fort Wayne students were moved to join with Walther and the St. Louis students on the St. Louis campus. It was thought to be a more economical way of educating church workers. It was also hoped that in the presence of the St. Louis faculty the Fort Wayne "practical" seminarians could be exposed to a more sophisticated education. Originally Loehe had hoped to move the Fort Wayne seminarians to Columbus, Ohio. However, later Loehe decided to sever his connections with the Columbus school and rather to work with Walther and LC—MS.

C. The LC—MS Ministerial Education System Develops

Cramer and Walther actually worked together on the St. Louis campus for fourteen years, retaining two separate paths into the ministry. The practical seminarians were at first designated as "catechetes" who were placed into congregations working under the guidance of full-fledged pastors.

1. Springfield

In August 1873 the "Practical" seminary students with their leader Cramer were moved to Springfield, Ill. Here they continued their own program while the St. Louis seminary provided a more extensive theoretical program including, especially, training in the original biblical languages. Entrance requirements of the "practical" seminary were raised progressively to high school graduates. Eventually, under Springfield President Beto, entrance requirement for the Springfield seminary became almost the same as those of St. Louis.

The desire for Synod to retain two seminaries, fairly similar in their programs was often questioned and debated. At the Saginaw convention in 1935 Synod actually voted to close the Springfield seminary. However, a groundswell of opposition grew into reconsidering the decision the following day and voting not to close it.

35

2. Prep Schools

Meanwhile, the six year gymnasium program, modeled after the European training which the founding synodical pastors had received, was retained as a St. Louis seminary entrance requirement. Sometimes questions arose about doing what other protestant denominations were doing, namely, requiring a four year college degree for seminary entrance. The memory of the German university liberalism which had originally brought the founding pastors to move to America was strong enough to retain the "gymnasium" program as a sufficient seminary entrance requirement for LC—MS pastors.

In fact, the original Fort Wayne "college" eventually led to a whole system of "prep" schools in Milwaukee, St. Paul, Concordia, Missouri, Winfield, Bronxville, Portland, Oakland, and Austin. This system of "prep" schools remained the preferred route in LC—MS until the establishment of the Senior college in Fort Wayne in 1957. Even then, by compromise, they retained the "gymnasium" six year system for a time and let the upper two senior college years become the bridge leading to the St. Louis seminary.

CHAPTER 5

To Change or Not to Change the LC—MS Ministerial Education System

A. The German Lutheran Church in America (1838-1917)

1. The Early Twofold Thrust into America

In grade school I learned that the Missouri Synod began with the activity of the Saxon fathers in Perry County, Missouri and in St. Louis. That understanding was strongly reinforced during my studies at Concordia Seminary, St. Louis. Not until recently did I realize that LC-MS's outreach had a twofold thrust, one from Perry County and St. Louis and the other from Fort Wayne, Indiana. Actually, St. Paul's congregation, the mother of Lutheranism in Fort Wayne was organized in 1837, two years before the Saxon fathers arrived in St. Louis and Perry County.

C.F.W. Walther, with his "Lutheraner" drew Lutherans from Indiana, Ohio, Michigan, Illinois and other areas into the discussions of gathering congregations together into a Synod. A number of preliminary meetings, including the one in which a constitution was written for the new synod which was officially established in Chicago in 1847. A predominance of congregations from Fort Wayne and Adams County, Indiana were charter member of the Synod which they named "The Evangelical Lutheran Church of Missouri, Ohio and other States."

Regardless of where the original congregations of LC-MS were located, they were all German. Though they did not include the word German in their official name, they all clearly stated in their local constitutions that they were German. Both seminaries, the one that had started in St. Louis as well as the one which Wyneken and Sihler and Loehe started in Fort Wayne clearly stated that they wanted the teaching to be in German. The stated purpose and mission of the Synod was to gather together the scattered German Lutherans who had immigrated into America

37

into congregations and to train pastors to serve them and their families.

2. The German Lutheran Church, officially known as the Missouri Synod, was also predominantly Midwestern and rural. With the exception of congregations in St. Louis, Chicago, and Milwaukee, most of the congregations were either located among families living on their farms or in small towns in which the Lutheran farmers did their business and retired. German Lutheran immigrants moved westward into Ohio, Indiana, and Michigan and Northward from Perry County and St. Louis to settle in and to till the vast mid western farmlands.

A second wave of European immigration came toward the end of the nineteenth century. That's when the mission work of the Missouri Synod was busy gathering German Lutherans as they settled in the farms and small towns of Illinois, Wisconsin, Minnesota, Iowa, the Dakotas and Nebraska. During these years the church's energies and funds were expended in forming congregations, establishing more and more junior colleges (including high schools) to provide pre-seminary education for German-speaking pastors and refining teacher training at River Forest and Seward to prepare teachers for parochial schools. The children who went through their parochial schools learned their religion in German and the secular subjects, reading, writing and arithmetic, in English. The families with their growing American children largely spoke German at home and in church, and moved slowly into the use of English when they did their business in small bilingual towns. And so the German Lutheran congregations were not only the religious centers but also the German cultural centers of their communities. There was a strong tendency for German immigrants to form closed communities.

Lutherans who had immigrated to America before the western expansion were different from Midwestern rural people. Midwesterners tended to be seclusive if not clannish, while easterners interacted with their American neighbors. Thus, the earlier eastern Lutherans moved away from narrow German ways and theology and imitated non-Lutheran tendencies. To put it briefly, eastern Lutherans were more liberal and Midwestern Lutherans were staunchly conservative.

The rural predominance also subtly led to an anti intellectual attitude. For one thing, every possible laborer was necessary to help with the farm work. That meant that its boys and girls needed to stay home from school so they could help with field work. As a result, many boys and girls were never really able to finish the eighth grade much less think of attending high school. This lack of school experience carried over into family and church decision making.

B. Forces that Brought Change (1917-1923)

1. Third and fourth generation American-born Lutherans over time brought interesting changes to Lutheran families and congregations. As the public school elementary education improved in American public schools it had an effect on German Lutheran parochial schools. Young people became increasingly bilingual and helped their parents to do the same. In the communities where they lived children and young people interacted more and more with their peers both German and non-German. This brought American culture to interact with and to influence the German culture which had formerly been characteristic of isolated Lutheran groups described in the previous section. To a limited extent, even marriages between Lutherans and non-Lutherans became more and more common and influenced the thought and lifestyles in the congregations where they occurred.

2. Word War I brought international thought and influence upon German Lutheran congregations. In some communities non-German neighbors looked with suspicion upon their German neighbors. Increasing influence of the state public school systems also exerted their influence upon the parochial schools of German Lutheran congregations. In some states the public school system insisted upon more use of the English language than had been the case earlier. This made it difficult for some of the teachers and especially the German speaking pastors who also taught school in their congregations. In addition there was a new attitude that was brought into their home congregations when members who had served in the military forces against

Germany returned home after the war. Thus, there was an ever increasing pressure by the young people in the country, the small towns, and especially in the larger city congregations to Americanize their churches.

C. A Deliberate Push to Upgrade Pre-Seminary Education for LC—MS Pastors (1923-1947)

More and more people asked questions about the LC-MS pre-ministerial education system. A few clergy wanted to know why they couldn't have a B.A. besides a seminary diploma. Returning soldiers and some campus pastors wanted to know why we were so different from other protestant churches. Some public school teachers and administrators as well as pharmacists, doctors and lawyers also wondered. And even a few professors from the synodical junior colleges spoke up.

1. Actual Proposal for Change to LC—MS Convention (1923)

By 1923 some daring innovative souls suggested that the soon to become vacant old seminary in south St. Louis might be an inexpensive place to start an upper level college for LC-MS pre-seminary students. They actually sent a memorial to the 1923 convention requesting this. The request was not voted down but tabled.

2. Professors' Conference Petitions Synod to Add Two College Years To Pre-seminary Ministerial Education (1926)

Discussion at the 1923 convention indicated enough interest in the subject to encourage the "prep" school professors to restudy the question more thoroughly and to come with a new memorial to Synod. So at their meeting in Lombard, Ill., in June 1925, the Professors' Conference resolved to petition the Hon. Synod "to add two years to our junior college course, thus extending it to a senior college and placing it on a par with that of our American colleges, without indeed losing sight of our peculiar needs."

Among the reasons they gave for this drastic proposed change they said: "a) That our students may be better prepared for the study of theology and for the office of the ministry, b) That our students may be of more advanced age and of firmer character when they enter St. Louis, c) That our future pastor may attain a greater knowledge and with perfect right may be considered college graduates (A. B. degree), e) That pastors who must also teach school may on the basis of their credits, receive a state certificate of teaching, f) That we ourselves may give our students that education, under Christian influence, which some now seek in other institutions with great danger for the welfare of their souls and for the Church."

The conference proposed using the vacated old seminary buildings in St. Louis, beginning in the fall of 1926. This would save the cost of building new facilities. It would also immediately remove the senior college students from the junior college campuses, separating them from the influence of high school students. Using the vacant St. Louis seminary building was to be temporary. After about six years, they suggested that a central senior college campus could be built. The Professors' conference showed their seriousness about this need by asking for a unanimous vote.

A similar memorial was also presented to Synod by the Western District.

However, a Memorial from a Lake Superior Special Conference opposed the idea. They argued as follows: "a) The idea was impractical, b) Synod was not sufficiently prepared for this step, c) This would require the cost of additional professors, an appropriate library, modern scientific laboratories, d) The church must confine to a minimum of scientific knowledge— Christ added only one learned Paul to His group, the rest were mostly simple fishermen—, and e) An academic degree when men enter the ministry is of minor importance. "

The 1926 LC—MS convention decided:

a) Although many reasons spoke for the adoption of the position, the matter be deferred to the next convention, especially for financial reasons, and

b) That the President appoint a committee which is to weigh the serviceability of the proposals contained in the memorial, make appropriate recommendations respecting ways and means of carrying out the plan, and see to it that our congregations are sufficiently informed as to this matter.

3. Professors' Conference Petitions Synod to Add a Year of College to each of six Junior Colleges (1929)

The Professors' Conference assembled at Hinsdale, Ill., in July, 1928, "again petitions the Ven. Synod to grant an extension of our six-year course of study which prepares students to enter the Seminary." The Professors' Conference has expressed itself, after due consideration, as opposed to the plan of creating a Central Senior College, either on the old Seminary site or elsewhere, and petitions to extend in this manner: a) An additional year to be added to the present course of study at six preparatory schools, namely, Bronxville, Concordia, Fort Wayne, Milwaukee, St. Paul, Winfield, b) Two schools each year, beginning September, 1930.

Reasons: "a. Cost to Synod is low, b. Cost to students is kept at its lowest point (less travel), c. Present school-buildings and plants would be used more fully, d. Synod eventually needs several educational pivots, e. Avoids sudden large decrease in seminary graduates, f. Since it would add only slightly to the enrollment of each school, it would help retain a highly intimate contact between students and faculty, g. student would attend only two different schools as he becomes a pastor."

4. Fort Wayne Pastoral Conference proposes a thorough study by a special committee (Synod adopted this in 1929)

"a. Cause a thorough study of our entire educational system for the theoretical training reshaping it so that it will better meet our aims and at the same time create a four year accredited college and a four year accredited high school

b. Have Synod appoint a committee of seven (one St. Louis prof, one Springfield prof, one junior college prof, two pastors, two laymen (preferably American educators):

—to engage experts in educational surveying to make an academic and administrative survey of our junior colleges in next three years

—to confer with these experts on the best ways and means of reshaping our educational program for ministers

—make recommendations available to conferences and interested bodies by January 1931

—present a complete report with specific recommendations to the next Synodical convention

—Make $10,000 to $15,000 available to pay these experts."

SYNODICAL ACTION:

Synod adopted the report of committee 1 "Your committee recommends that Synod instruct the President in conjunction with the vice-presidents to appoint a committee of nine from our own circles to survey the entire educational situation on the basis of these overtures and report to the next Synod

"We furthermore recommend that this committee send a report to the conferences of Synod one year prior to the next convention."

5. Pastors' Conference of Fort Wayne Submits Memorial (1932)

The Pastoral Conference of Fort Wayne and Vicinity submits memorial 124 with recommendations relative to the necessary expansion of our theoretical ministerial education: a. Retain the present junior-college system, b. Establish one senior college (junior and senior collegiate years) at St. Louis as an undergraduate department of the Seminary, using for the present the old Seminary building, c. Appoint a committee to work out transition and curriculum.

WHY EXPAND COLLEGE TO FOUR YEARS?

a. Life is growing increasingly complex and pastoral problems are becoming more complicated.

b. Educational level of American people is constantly rising. Educational standards of other professions (law, medicine, engineering, education, etc.) have greatly increased in past decades.

c. Members of congregations are attending universities in growing numbers.

d. Increasingly cultured audiences demand more culture from its pastors.

e. Departments of learning (physical sciences, psychology, education, sociology, etc.) which have important bearing on theology, cannot even be surveyed with only a two year college program.

f. Present ministerial education program has been severely criticized by many in Synod.

g. German has become a practically foreign language at Synod's junior colleges

WHY RETAIN JUNIOR-COLLEGE SYSTEM UNCHANGED

a. Four years high school and two years college now exists in more than 400 American schools

b. Reducing schools to academies only will cause their gradual decay

c. We need the upper class-men (Prima and Secunda) to help supervise the students in four lower classes.

d. We've had a favorable experience with our six-year schools over the years.

WHY ONE SENIOR COLLEGE?

a. Simplicity, b. Complete development, c. Harmony, d. Studious atmosphere. (No downward pull by freshmen & sophomores), e. Flexibility, f. Conserving graduates, g. Economy.

Establishment of a senior college was also advocated in unprinted Memorial 84 submitted by the St. Louis faculty

SYNODICAL ACTION :

It was resolved to refer this matter to the Committee on Higher Education

6. Committee On Higher Education Reports Five Possible Plans (1935)

REPORT OF THE COMMITTEE ON HIGHER EDUCATION

A. Objectives of Ministerial Training

a. Development of Christian character, personality, and Christian leadership

b. A thorough knowledge of the Bible and of the four branches of theology

c. Ability to write and speak an idiomatic and forceful English; a reading, writing, and fairly good speaking knowledge of German; a reading knowledge of Latin, Greek, and Hebrew

d. An understanding of the modern world through courses in the natural and the social sciences

e. A reasonable acquaintance with, interest in, and appreciation of the humanities ((literary and other artistic products)

f. Development of the ability to think clearly and properly, to analyze, organize, and present the acquired material

B. Need of an improved ministerial education

It is highly necessary for the pastor to understand the world in which he lives, so that he can apply the Word of God to the specific needs of his people. Cf. Memorial 124 by Pastoral Conference of Fort Wayne and Vicinity

C. How to Achieve Such Adjustment and Improvement.
FIVE PLANS:

a. Add two years to one or more of our present junior colleges

b. Establish one or more four year colleges and reduce our other institutions to academies or high schools

c. Eliminate high school departments in present junior colleges and add third and fourth year to all colleges, making them all four year colleges

d. Establish one central senior college, with the third and fourth years of the standard college course, and to retain our junior colleges as feeders to this institution

e. Retain our present six-year combination of high school and junior college and to add one pre-theological year to the course of the seminary at St. Louis

The committee recommends plan five and rejects the first four."We therefore respectfully recommend the retention of our present system of six-year junior colleges with a revised curriculum and the addition of a pre-theological to our course at the seminary at St. Louis.

Reasons: a. This plan is conservative, b. This plan is progressive, c. This plan is economical for Synod

SYNODICAL ACTION:

RESOLVED:

1. That we retain our present system of ministerial education, revise the high-school and junior college curriculum, and add one year to our course in the Seminary in St. Louis.

2. Appoint a committee on Higher Education. It appoint a Committee on Curriculum

3. Committee on Higher Education to decide when the new plan is to go into effect and is to supervise the introduction of this new curriculum

Committee on Higher Education to make definite recommendations to the next convention on the library facilities needed.

Grant a Bachelor's Degree after the successful completion of the first two years at St. Louis.

7. Synod Establishes a Board for Higher Education (1938)

SYNODICAL ACTION:

It was resolved that the present Committee on Higher Education continue in office and be empowered to function until the new Board for Higher Education is ready to take over the work.

8. Board for Higher Education Recommends Survey of the Entire Synodical Ministerial Education System. (1941)

This brought about the Hausman study and report.

9. After the Hausman report, Synod asks the Board for Higher Education to further study and bring a report and recommendation to the Centennial Convention in Chicago (1944)

SYNODICAL ACTION:

"The Board for Higher Educations was requested to make further studies regarding the advisability of changing over to a four-year college course in preparation for entrance to a three-year course in theology in St. Louis and to submit a report with recommendations to Synod in 1947."

CHAPTER 6

The Centennial Decision to Change

Ever since 1923 Synod had been struggling with the question about adding two years of college, leading to a B. A. degree, to the "gymnasium" (four years high school plus two years of college) "prep" school system which had become the standard entrance requirement for the three year theological program at the seminary in St. Louis.

A. Creation of Position: Executive Secretary of Board for Higher Education

Professors' conferences, pastors' conferences, committees, consultants, surveys plus the Hausman report to the Saginaw convention in 1944 finally brought the matter to a turning point. The Board for Higher Education, established a permanent full

Dr. Martin J. Neeb—Executive Secretary of
The Board for Higher Education and
First President of Concordia Senior College.

47

time position known as the Executive Secretary of the Board for Higher Education. That position would pull together ideas about training ministers and teachers under a single qualified educational expert and grant authority to supervise and recommend necessary changes for growth and development.

That position, created by Synod at the Saginaw Convention in 1944, led to the extension of a call to The Rev. Martin J. Neeb. He accepted the call in September, 1945. He established his office in Chicago on January 1, 1946.

Martin Neeb personally had gone through the LC—MS ministerial education system with his attendance and graduation from the "prep" school in Fort Wayne and the St. Louis Seminary. In addition, he had served as a faculty member of Synod's "prep" school at Austin, Texas. He also came to his new position with a master's degree in education from the University of Texas. His experience and interest had prepared him well for the challenging task of thoroughly studying Synod's ministerial education system, of analyzing the history and many proposals which had been referred to the new Board for Higher Education and bringing recommendations, as requested by Saginaw in 1944, to the Centennial Synodical Convention scheduled for Chicago.

His 54 page printed report to the Chicago convention is a beautiful example of his expertise and thoroughness. Listening to him on the floor of the convention quickly demonstrated that he was a man who knew what he was talking about, who was convinced of the validly of his findings, and who possessed the persuasive skills which could get the convention to make a decision.

From the time that Neeb took charge in January, 1946 to the time of the 1947 convention in June, the Board for Higher Education had talked about changing the pre-ministerial ministerial education system.. Neeb also had two sessions with Synod's board of directors, five with the Advisory Council (College and Seminary presidents), one with the Professors' Conference and one joint session with the Board for Parish Education. He also spent time seeking to coordinate Synod's "prep" schools, a task which had become more complicated by the demands for more and more general education by the various schools, and by the adjustments which resulted from the Hausman report.

B. Idea of a Senior College

With the help of special committees, many church and secular consultants, the deliberation of the Professors' Conference, the Advisory Council, the Board for Higher Education had given prolonged and exhaustive study to the directive it had been given by the Saginaw convention.

1. Many Plans Offered

The various ideas, among others, which Neeb and others worked with included:

a. An expressed desire to adjust the Church's program of ministerial education so that in its mechanics it will parallel or duplicate current American Protestant practice in theological training and secular patterns of professional education.,

b. Suggestions that adjustments in the high school programs at the Preparatory Colleges be brought into conformity with the American pattern,

c. Reference to the difficulties which many military chaplains had experienced because they did not have a B. A. degree from a regionally accredited American college,

d. A conviction that today's ministry requires broader training in the social studies than it has been getting, and

e. Another group calls attention to increasing numbers of American Junior colleges.

2. Statement of Objectives of Ministerial Training

The Saginaw convention had directed The Board for Higher Education to formulate a statement of the fundamental objectives of ministerial training as a specific guide to Synod in the future operation of its Colleges and Seminaries.

Objectives were presented as follows:

A Students before entering the St. Louis Seminary should:
    a. Acquire a Doctrinal Knowledge
    b. Develop a Spiritually Dominated Personality

c. Acquire a Knowledge of Man

d. Acquire appropriate Personal Habits, Skills and Attitudes

e. Acquire An Appreciation of the Minister's Functions as an integral part of the Lutheran Church

C. Practical Implications

Clearly, this approach to a study of our ministerial education system required that all schools needed to state their objectives with as much precision and with as much completeness as possible. Special emphasis also needed to be placed upon the objectives which describe the development of the student's personality in directions other than merely intellectual and placed great stress upon definite spiritual achievements. We needed to avoid the error of confusing ends and means. This also includes all phases of the student's experiences including extra-curricular influences. A serious attempt to make the objectives effective would impose certain requirements upon: a. Administrators, b. Teachers, c. School equipment, and d. the curriculum.

1. A quick review of our past.

We have followed a policy of segregated training with specialized curricula. There has been a sharp focus on a single objective.There's room for improvement especially in those areas of training which attempt practical adaptation to the constantly changing world conditions which confront us and that have always challenged the preacher's capacity for adjustment of method and technique.

There have already been gradual and subtle changes in our colleges during the past century of service. Changes in basic language of instruction, in curriculum, in administration, in guidance, in the admission of students at higher levels, and in the introduction of general education. There's been a rapid development of urbanization and mechanization in American life which tends to make the task of ministry increasingly difficult. Servants of the Church must be so trained as to be able to understand the moving currents of human thought and action, and also know

50

how to bring the Word of God to bear upon the personal and collective problems of the world in which we live.

2. General Education

A basic modification of traditional objectives has introduced a large number of non-ministerial students into Synod's system of schools. General education absorbs about 50% of all available preparatory facilities. The objectives of general education and of ministerial education are basically not the same.

The Board for Higher Education believes that a Senior College devoting its facilities exclusively to pre-ministerial curricula and a program of ministerial training is the best answer to the problem.

3. Functions of the Senior College

a. The first and dominant function of the proposed Senior College is to serve as a carefully planned and thoroughly organized program which candidates for the Seminary in St. Louis may experience. This includes: a profound strengthening of their Christian faith, a deepening of their consecration to Christ, and a genuine and wholesome development of their personal sanctification.

b. The cultivation of desirable intellectual traits and viewpoints, for the sake of discipline.

c. The extension of the cultural knowledge of the student (courses now in the first seminary year and a comprehensive major in the field of the social sciences.)

d. Consciously undertaking the development of the student's personality, especially in the area of social habits and social attitudes, so as to form a socially competent Christian gentleman.

e. Graduation with a B. A. degree.

D. The Decision

1. Many Proposals

In all there were 18 different proposals for changing the LC—MS ministerial education system. These were studied and out of them a total of six were presented for consideration. These were:

a. Build a new college,

b. Adapt a preparatory school (Fort Wayne, Milwaukee, St. Paul),

c. Make four-year colleges out of Bronxville, Fort Wayne, and Oakland,

d. Establish a four year pre-ministerial college at Seward and River Forest,

e. Send graduates from junior colleges to Valparaiso for two years and a B.A. degree,

f. Establish a pre-ministerial Valparaiso extension on the River Forest Campus, or

g. Place a Senior College on the St. Louis Seminary Campus.

2. Recommendations:

a. It was recommended that Synod establish a Senior College as an additional unit in the professional training of ministerial students. (The term "Senior College" is understood to designate the academic level of the junior and senior years of the standard American college.) This recommendation included the following:

(1). That the present Junior College system be retained

(2). That the curriculum of the present Junior College and the proposed Senior College be completely articulated and integrated and that the same degree of co-ordination be established between the entire College program and the program of the Seminary.

(3). That the changes necessary in the present Junior College program to achieve complete articulation and integration of the Junior and Senior divisions be authorized

(4). That efforts toward securing regional accreditation of the ministerial academies and Junior Colleges be accelerated during the next trienium.

b. That the Board for Higher Education be directed to continue its study to determine a satisfactory location for the Senior College as well as its organization, curriculum, and plant requirement.

(1). That upon completion of these studies the Board be directed to formulate plans for location, organization, curriculum, and physical plant of the Senior College and to submit these preliminary plans together with its recommendations to the Synodical Convention of 1950

(2). That any costs occasioned by the preparation and presentation of such preliminary plans be approved for payment as items separate from the regular budget of the Board for Higher Education.

3. SYNODICAL ACTION:

Upon recommendation of Floor committee 1 it was resolved:

a. That Synod establish a senior college (on the level of the junior and senior years of the American college system) as an additional unit in its program of the professional training of ministerial students.

(1). That Synod's high school-junior college system be retained

(2). That the curriculum of our high school-junior college, with any necessary changes, be integrated with that of the proposed senior college and that the curriculum of the senior college, or its equivalent, be a prerequisite for entrance into the St. Louis seminary.

a. That efforts toward securing regional accreditation of the ministerial academies and junior colleges be accelerated during the next trienium so as to facilitate accreditation of the proposed senior college.

b. That the Board for Higher Education be directed to continue its study to determine a satisfactory location for the senior college as well as its organization, curriculum, and plant requirements.

(1). That upon completion of these studies the Board for Higher Education be instructed to formulate the above plans and to submit them together with its recommendations to the next synodical convention.

(2). That any cost occasioned by the preparation and presentation of such preliminary plans be approved for payment as items separate from the regular budget of the Board for Higher Education.

Thus, the ministerial education system which the Lutheran Church—Missouri Synod had used for a century is to be changed. The four year high school, two year college (modeled after the

53

German "gymnasium" university program) was to become a four year high school, two year junior college, and a two year senior college.

This would bring the system from what the founders had brought with them from Germany closer to the Protestant ministerial programs of America.

CHAPTER 7

Planning and Building the Scandinavian Village 1947-1957

A. The 1950 Milwaukee Convention—
Planning the Senior College

At the 1950 convention in Milwaukee BHE reported to Synod: "After studying many factors over a period of the past five years the Board is still convinced that Synod was entirely correct when at the Centennial Convention it resolved to progress toward giving its ministers full college training." Since that indicated considerable reluctance and opposition on the part of many, pastors and lay people, to the drastic change which was voted in Chicago in 1947. Dr. Neeb and BHE had to spend considerable time listening to the opposition and finding ways to counteracting it.

They did this by helping people to realize what was happening in the country around them and in all of the vocations with which lay and pastoral delegates were daily interacting and for which they and their families were preparing their own children to grow into. In other words they needed to help people stop living only in the the past, to move into the present, and to look forward to the future.

The BHE report indicated that: "the college population in the USA had increased about 1000% between 1900 and 1948." LC-MS members needed to realize that the educational progress of Synod's membership parallels that of the general American public.

"Having, therefore, a clear sense of the direction in which we must go, a conviction that our need is real, and the mathematical evidence that our immediate action is required to achieve desirable results a decade hence, there remains the need for a decision on initiating a program which will eventually lead us to the desired goals"With that introduction BHE proceeded to talk about plans:

1. Basic Assumptions:

a. Withdraw one year from the present four-year seminary course.

b. Seminary curriculum will be almost wholly professional

c. Students entering seminary need to adequately possess the spiritual and personality development as well as the technical and intellectual apparatus necessary for a high level of professional training.

d. All of the objectives of the four-year senior college curriculum need to have the single aim of equipping young men to enter the seminary.

e. Senior college, rather than only an upper level liberal arts college needs, specifically, to prepare men to enter the seminary.

f. This requires a single curriculum, highly prescribed, with a limited opportunity to elect

g. Even special interest choices need to prepare for work in the church.

h. Any additional special training needs to be acquired at another university.

i. The curriculum is not the entire but only one of the educational experiences the CSC student needs to acquire.

2. Suggested Aims:

a. Expand the student's knowledge of the Word.

b. Help the student to thoroughly understand man. Observe the product of heredity and also of a dynamic social environment. Requires a study of the science of society and the science of psychology.

c. Understand relationship of the history of the Church with the history of the world.

d. Develop high language skills

e. Establish a reasonable foundation in philosophy

f. Provide a basic appreciation of education.

3. Spiritual Grown and Maturation are Essential

Student needs to thoroughly know and sincerely believe God's revealed truths to be able accurately to distinguish between divine truth and human error, and manifest the Christian faith in an exemplary spiritual life.

a. Students need to acquire a more highly developed spiritual strength and sensitivity

b. Develop an adequate spiritual personality

4. Accreditation

Accreditation is highly important as early as possible.

5. Senior College Curriculum

This should include Religion, Church history, Latin, Greek, Hebrew, German, Social Sciences, English and Literature, Philosophy, Education, and Psychology.

6. Administrative Organization

a. The President
b. Dean of Students
c. The Registrar
d. The Business Manager
e. The Librarian
f. The Instructional Staff: First year: Call five and appoint five. Second year: add as needed All called men initially rank: Associate Professors or Full professors.
g. Service staff: Two full time clerical, add as needed

7. Procedure

a. Cite selection
b. Building placement
c. Appoint interim local board of control
d. BHE empowered to develop initial curriculum of CSC
e. Temporary policies: Elections and/or appointments

8. Location

Chicago, Detroit, St. Louis, St. Paul. Final Decision to be made by Synod's Presidium, District Presidents, Board of Directors, and BHE.

9. Cost:

$2,750,000 Annual operating cost approximately $200,000

10. BHE recommendations to Milwaukee Convention:

a. That Synod give BHE authority to execute senior college plan approved by the convention

b. That Synod gives BHE authority to make adjustments to to junior college and seminary program as required by Synod's plan

c. That Synod authorize Board of Directors and Fiscal Conference to provide funds

SYNODICAL ACTION:

a. Resolved: "That we proceed to carry out our resolutions of 1947 to establish a Senior College in accordance with the proposals submitted to Synod by BHE."

b. Resolved "That the final decision on the location of the Senior College be made by the President of Synod, the Board of Directors, BHE, the District Presidents, and lay delegates appointed by each district (The 99)"

c. Resolved "That the sum of $2,750,000 be considered the approximate maximum amount (not including the possible cost of land)"-

B. The 1953 Houston Convention—Financing Concordia Senior College

Committee 1 presented a resolution, which was thoroughly discussed and adopted almost unanimously:

1. Pause: Insufficient Funds

The Milwaukee convention reaffirmed the decision of 1947 to establish a Senior College. Choice of location Synod left to the Committee of 99 (Presidium, District Presidents, layman from each District, Synod's Board of Directors, BHE, with presidents of colleges and seminaries as advisory members) Committee of 99 decided to locate in Chicago or Milwaukee suburban area.

BHE asked Synod's Board of Directors to take options and get an architect. Board. of Directors asked BHE not to proceed until Houston Convention. The $3,000,000 approved was not enough. Besides many people believed adding another campus was not good stewardship and some felt that a four-year Senior College would be more desirable.

2. An Offer to Sell Fort Wayne Junior College

Meanwhile an unsolicited offer came from Indiana Technical College to buy the old Fort Wayne campus for $1,000,000. Previously the Junior College had been given authority to build a Library and an Administration building on the old campus for $335,000. The combined sale plus the authorized buildings would provided an additional $1,335,000 to the $3,000,000 authorized budget to build a Senior college.

a. Advantages listed for the sale:

(1). Avoids establishing another campus.

(2). Provides sufficient funds to construct a Senior College

(3). Avoids spending money on an old campus.

(4). Would locate Senior College in a high Lutheran population area.

b. Disadvantages:

(1). Chicago or Milwaukee provides better off-campus opportunities like: libraries, cultural facilities, opportunities for faculty graduate studies.

(2). Authorized Fort Wayne Junior College Experiment would need to be located elsewhere

(3). Fort Wayne teacher-training program would need to be transferred elsewhere

(4). Chicago provides better transportation opportunities than Fort Wayne

After considering pros and cons, the committee recommends selling the old campus and making the $1,000,000 available to add to Senior College cost budget.

Many considered the Indiana Tech offer providential, suggesting that, therefore, the previous Committee of 99 decision should be changed. Besides, Fort Wayne location does not prevent a possible additional Senior College or changing the senior college to a four-year school.

Tracing the history of the Fort Wayne College from Perry County to St. Louis, to Fort Wayne, to a preparatory school, a seminary, and a teacher-training school. Placing the Senior College in Fort Wayne would be the hallowed historical succession.

SYNODICAL ACTION (Adopted almost unanimously):

a. That Synod construct, equip, and furnish a two-year Senior College in Fort Wayne or its suburban area.

b. That Synod sell the Fort Wayne Junior college to Indiana Technical College for $1,000,000

c. That the original $3,000,000 authorization plus the Junior College sale for $1,000,000 plus the $335,000 allocated to the Fort Wayne Junior College be combined to provide a total of $4,335,000 to build the Senior College in Fort Wayne.

d. That faculty housing costs to be excluded from this budget.

e. That the 4.86 acres which Concordia High School had been renting from Synod be given to Fort Wayne Concordia Lutheran High School Association for the sum of $1.

C. The 1956 St. Paul Convention:
Concordia Senior College under Construction

1. Fort Wayne Junior College Sale

BHE immediately began to carry out the 1953 resolution: They sold the Fort Wayne Junior College. They began building Concordia Senior College in Fort Wayne. Progress reports were made to synodical Districts in 1954 and 1955 at District Conventions. There were also reports and a special column in the Lutheran Witness giving progress reports.

2. Site Selection

After a five month search a 177 acre farm was bought from Howard Kramer and a 10 acre corner from George Sweet. This was located between Highway 427 (now Clinton Street) and the St. Joseph River.

3. Architect Selection

The Board chose an architect of of the highest professional competence in the person of Eero Saarinen. This happened June 23, 1953. Saarinen reported to Synod's Fiscal conference in 1954 describing the site, the buildings planned, and their location.

Dr. Behnken, Pres. LC-MS, Mr. Eero Saarinen, Dr. Birkner, Sec. LC-MS, Dr. Neeb, Exec. Sec. BHE

Building capacities were: chapel 600, library 150, 10 classrooms of 33 each, lecture room 125, speech department with individual and group practice rooms, 3 counselors' offices, auditorium 510, dining room 492, gymnasium bleachers 1,800 plus 1200 chairs on gym floor, 13 dormitories each housing 34 in double rooms, 1 small private study, one lounge, one prayer chapel.

4. Financial Limit

As planning progressed it became clear that the finances authorized in 1949, 1950, and 1953 would not be sufficient to build the entire campus. This left three alternatives: a. Postpone all building until after St. Paul (1956) Convention, b. Build as

61

much of the campus as authorized money made possible, or c. Construct only those facilities which are needed for the first year of operation up to limit of $5,200,000 before St. Paul Convention in June 1956.

5. Dr. Martin J. Neeb elected President

Meanwhile the Board. of Control got nominations for president. Dr. Neeb was elected and accepted the call. Now the board could proceed with staffing. They wanted to open school in fall of 1956 but this was delayed until 1957.

Neeb was In touch with North Central Association. The new institution was invited to apply for accreditation when it was about ready to graduate its second class.

The Board for Higher Education recommended that Synod authorize funds necessary to complete the campus and its facilities.

SYNODICAL ACTION:

a) Commend Board of Directors, BHE, Board of Control of CSC, College of Presidents for "their vision and action in providing for the completion of CSC

b) Urge the earliest possible completion and opening CSC in Fort Wayne, IN.

c) Ratify repeated interim actions taken by various boards

d) Authorize the necessary funds—not to exceed a total of $7,150,000

e) Have the president of Synod ask pastors and congregations of Synod to offer special prayers of thanksgiving.

Authority to finish building and opening Concordia Senior College in Fort Wayne, Indiana was given by the Syndical Convention in St. Paul, Minn. in 1956.

In September 1957 the first year class began at Concordia Senior College.

Groundbreaking, May, 1954.

Chapel Construction during first schoolyear.

63

First CSC faculty meeting, January, 1957.

Installation of original CSC faculty, at St. Paul's.

64

Aerial View (looking northeast) of completed campus.

Dining Hall Interior

Upper Plaza, Looking West.

**Prof. Walle completes registration of first student,
Mr. George Marquart.**

**Campus Dedication (after chapel construction
had been completed), May, 1958.**

CHAPTER 8

Concordia Senior College Takes Off in the Scandinavian Village (1957-1977)

A. Staffing

1. Administration:

President, Martin J. Neeb
Academic Dean, Walter Wente
Registrar, Oscar Walle
Dean of Students, Richard Jesse
Librarian, Lando Otto
Dean of Administration, Herbert G. Bredemeier
Business Manager, Edgar Walz
Athletic Director/Coach, Wilbert Stelzer

2. Faculty, First Two Academic Years

1955	1956	1957	1958
Neeb	Bartling	Bente	Hillers
	Essig	Bertram	Kriefall
	Harms	Bredemeier	Maleske
	Hermes	Coates	Malte
	Jesse	Graesser	Mundinger
	Otto	Haas, H	Schroeder
	Walle	Haas. R.	Spomer
	Wente	Meyer, E	Stegemoeller
		Meyer, J.	
		Nissen	
		Nuechterlein	
		Schnabel	
		Schroeter	
		Stelzer	
		Walz	

3. Secretaries:

Esther Koehlinger-Pres. Neeb
Nancy Hartman-Dean of Students-Jesse
Betty Johnson-Dean of Administration-Bredemeier
Diane Schrock-Academic Dean-Wente
Ruth Nuss-Business Manager-Walz
Trudy Behning-Registrar-Walle
Elaine Soughan-Receptionist-Business Office
Velma Dutton-Bookkeeper-Business Office
Alice Doeden-Faculty Office
Dorothy Brandenburg-Faculty Office
William Brandenburg-Central Supplies Manager
Art Schmidt-Asst. Business Manager

4. Bookstore:

Ida Ernsting-Manager
Esther Walz-Part time helper
Paul Hanke-Student manager
Lloyd Strelow-Student helper
Robert Kuhn-Student helper

5. Maintenance

a. Grounds:
   Herbert Buesching-Manager
   Helpers: Koenig, Terry, Hemsoth, Wolf
b. Buildings:
   Elmer Grote-Manager
   Helpers: Sexton, Mrs. Winkler, Kramer. Elwood,
   Schuelke, Burry, Isenhower, Martin

6. Dining Hall:

Mr. & Mrs. Ed. Liedke operate Carmi Food Service
STAFF: Bill Ross, Herb Meinzen, Martha Ambrose, Olive
Kirchner, Janet Lynch, Margaret Wolfe, Lydia Meinzen,
Edna Frownfelter, Katherine Stein.

7. Infirmary:

> Mrs. John Meyer & Mrs. Paul Schroeder, faculty wives, serve as part-time nurses

B. Curriculum

Some idea of what would be taught at the Senior College had, of course, been included in the thinking and proposal to change the ministerial education system back in 1947. As development proceeded, Dr. Neeb, who was the Executive Secretary or the Board for Higher Education and later the first president of the Senior College, personally thought about the curriculum, and consulted frequently with the presidents and the faculty members of the junior colleges.

The specifics of the beginning curriculum, however, did not come into being until after president Neeb brought key faculty and administrators to Fort Wayne during 1956.

The LIBRARY was basic to any course and classroom activity. Therefore Prof. Lando Otto, Librarian and Miss Margaret Hermes, Assistant Librarian, were brought to Fort Wayne early in 1956 to begin establishing what would become the Library at the Senior College. Their first task was to examine every holding of the Fort Wayne Junior College library. They, personally, made the first decision about which book should be transferred to the Senior college library and which should be sent to the various libraries of Synods prep school system. As additional senior college faculty, such as administrators and department heads, came to Fort Wayne, they were also consulted.

Many of the Senior College courses were new. For these librarian Otto did extensive consulting with the department heads and other professors who were being added to the staff.

In addition to gathering library books, the two librarians also advised in regard to the furniture and equipment while the library was under construction. They also needed to determine policies and procedures and to set up a system of operation. By the time the school opened in September 1957, the library was ready to serve faculty and students.

71

Dr. Walter Wente, the ACADEMIC DEAN, had the challenging task of bringing a tentative curriculum, which had been worked out by the Curriculum Commission of the BHE, to the faculty.

C. Courses by Academic Quarters

Junior Year

First Quarter		Second Quarter		Third Quarter	
Christian Worship	2	Probl. of Christian		Literature Elective	4
Adv. Communications	3	Living	3	Movements of	
Movements of		Adv. Speech	3	Thought III	3
Thought I	3	Movements of		Growth and Develop-	
Human Body	3	Thought II	3	ment II	4
Language: Greek 105	2	Growth and Devel-		Language: Greek 107	2
German or Latin 105	2	opment I	4	German or Latin 106	2
	15		15		15

Elective	2 or 3	Elective	2 or 3		2 or 3

Senior Year

Christian Witness I	3	Christian Witness II	2	Concentration Elective	3
Concentration Elective	3	Concentration Elective	3	Soc. Sc.Elective II	3
Elective	2	Social Science Elec. I	3	Philosophy of Science	4
Language: Greek 208	2	Language: Greek 209	2	Language: Greek 210	2
German or Latin 207	2	German or Latin 208	2	Hebrew III	3
Hebrew I	3	Hebrew II	3		
	15		15		15

Elective	2 or 3		2 or 3		2 or 3

D. Faculty and Committee Meetings:

The first faculty meeting was held November 23, 1956 at the Gerber-Haus motel in Fort Wayne. Twelve were present. (See photo) The only resolution of this first faculty meeting was to express "acceptance of the basic required curriculum, as presented by the Academic Dean." (See above: Courses in Quarters)

Prof. Richard Jesse, DEAN OF STUDENTS, developed another important part of the program as he sketched a possible form of student government. He explained the community concept, the relationship and involvement of the resident counselors in a formal statement entitled "The Function and Form of the Senior College."

Meanwhile, Oscar Walle, THE REGISTRAR, developed the necessary preliminary structure of the registrar's office. He devised a system of records. He determined admissions procedures and policies.

During 1956 department heads and faculty in Fort Wayne also worked out specific course syllabi for all the courses that would be taught during the first school year.

In summary, with the adoption of the curriculum described above, four important changes from the previous synodical pre-ministerial system were established as follows: 1) Only German or Latin were required from a student 2) Each student was required to choose an area of concentration 3) During the junior year each student spends one course each term in the study of philosophy, and, 4) Two courses in psychology (Growth and Development I and II) would be required of each student during his junior year.

On May 12, 1957 nineteen faculty members were installed at a special service in St. Paul Lutheran Church, Fort Wayne. Administrators of Synod and of the Central District, BHE and the presidents of Synod's colleges and seminaries were present to participate in this special, historic occasion.

The faculty met many times before school opened in September. Meetings were held on May 13, and a preschool meeting on September 3 and 4. These pre- school meetings were inspiring, hard work, reporting and absorption of much information and organization. The accidental death of Prof. Paul Bente prior to the fall faculty meeting saddened the faculty and staff.

A most important part of the preschool meeting was the careful discussion of the college's objectives. These same objectives carried the college through its years of existence to its closing on June 30, 1977. They were:

"Concordia Senior College seeks to develop mature Christian personalities to whom knowledge and understanding of the Scriptures and Christian truth and of the history and functioning of the the church are joined with personal faith in Jesus Christ as God and Savior. Its resources are directed to the cultivation of Christian living and all Christian virtues and to the strengthening

73

of the ministerial student's intent to serve in the Lutheran ministry .

"In the academic program emphasis is placed on the development of sound habits of reasoning and judgment together with a high level of ability in the use of the English language for oral and written communication.

"A broad acquaintance with the chief fields of knowledge, i.e., the humanities, the social sciences, and the natural sciences, is to lead the student to an understanding of the world and of human nature and of basic problems of man and society.

"Special attention is given to the development in the ministerial student of proficiency in the use of foreign languages for theological study and research and for cultural enrichment.

"Habits and attitudes making for social competence and personal leadership: a discriminating understanding and appreciation of the cultural heritage in literature, music, and the fine arts, and the promotion and conservation of physical and mental health are matters of fundamental concern in the total program."

President Neeb's opening remarks in the September meeting:

"The instructor at Concordia Senior College must be more than an expert at explanation. He must be a model as a man and establish a relationship with students that has no barrier, and yet which prevents undue familiarity. The spirit of the community needs to apply to faculty-faculty relationships, to student-student relations, and to student-faculty contacts."

E. Student Government

On September 5 an advance group of twenty-nine student leaders arrived on campus. Each junior college had chosen these representatives to come. Under the leadership of the dean of students they began to work on a constitution for student government. Temporary officers were elected on Sept. 10 .

On Saturday and Sunday, Sept 7 and 8, the first class of students arrived on campus. On Monday and Tuesday, Sept 10 and 11 they went through orientation and registration.

The opening service was held on Monday, Sept. 10.

Classes for the fall term began on Wednesday, September 11, 1957. The Senior college was in session.

F. Notes about Photos

FIRST FACULTY MEETING OF CSC-11/23/1956-GERBER HAUS
Picture Spire Vol 1, 1959, p 12 (See Walle p 30)
Standing: Neeb, Harms, Walz
Seated: Otto, Bente, Wente, Bartling, Hermes, Bredemeier, Essig, Jesse, Walle.
FACULTY INSTALLATION, FT. WAYNE, ST. PAUL'S, 5/12/57
Picture Spire p 12.
Report and photo: Lutheran Witness 6/4/57 p 267
Installed: Neeb, See Luth Witness 6/4/57
FACULTY AT CSC OPENING, 9/10,57 SPIRE, VOL 1, P13
Neeb, Walle, Bredemeier, Otto, Wente,
Harms, J.Meyer,E. Meyer,Stelzer, R . Haas, Bertram, Essig, H. Haas, Nuechterlein, Coates, Schroeter, Walz, Schnabel, Bartling, Hermes.
"ADMINISTRATIVE TEAM" (Pre-school) Spire p. 11
Wente, Jesse, Bredemeier, Walle, Otto

Chapter 9

Concordia Senior College Rises to Its Height in the Scandinavian Village

A. Students and Faculty Bring Life to the Campus (1957-1959)

It was an historic occasion for everyone as twenty-three faculty and 195 students gathered for the opening service on Tuesday morning, September 19, 1957. Faculty and administrators had worked hard to get ready and students who came from 30 Synodical Districts were ready to go.

1. Adjusting to Fort Wayne

A few of the students, it is true, were wondering why they had to come here. They wanted to get into the ministry as quickly as possible. And now an additional year was forced upon them. Was this really necessary? If a Junior college diploma and four seminary years had done it all this time, why add another year? But Synod had decided to do it this way, so they had little choice.

For most students coming to Fort Wayne, Indiana was not an easy adjustment. They had spent six years in Milwaukee or St. Paul or Bronxville And now to come to a new Concordia campus in the undeveloped suburb of Fort Wayne was like coming to a school in the corn field. Many of them missed hustle of the city, and the culture and entertainment they had enjoyed. So, living "in the country" north of Fort Wayne was something to get used to.

Others desperately missed the presence of girls on campus. No cheerful voices around campus, in the dining room, in the classrooms. All male students, men professors. The only women on campus were the secretaries and the kitchen help and one lady on the maintenance staff. From the very beginning students wished there were some way to provide CSC with co-education. Girls in nurses' training at Lutheran and Parkview hospitals provided some opportunities for a social life. But things were not like they used to be in St. Paul or Bronxville.

The college tried hard to help with the social life. The hard winters did their best to provide good skating on the campus lake. Canadian and St. Paul students felt right at home with that. But the men who came from warmer parts of the country faced a frustrating challenge learning to appreciate winter sports. Hoosier basketball "hysteria" in Fort Wayne and Indiana high schools wasn't much help either.

Fortunately, the college had provided for a campus sports program. Intercollegiate wise, it is true, was quite challenging for the first year of an unknown small college. But they tried, with some success during the first year and better during the second. The high point of sports on the CSC campus was found in the intra- mural program. "Curly" Haas and "Pewee" Stelzer had the knack for providing participation opportunities for everyone. The small dormitories automatically grouped students into various opposing teams. So, student participation in basketball, tennis, baseball, golf and other sports was extensive. As had been hoped by administrators and faculty, this helped in student personality and relationship development.

Student government got off to a very good start. The various prep schools identified potential leaders in the advance representatives they had sent. Dean Jesse had the knack of getting student leaders involved early. The central officers, the dormitory representatives and the whole student spirit helped build a democratic system which helped to build character and leadership skills.

2. Taking Over a New Campus

Extensive glass doors on campus led to a minor problem on the first day of classes. Student Charles Bunzel tried to walk through a glass door and ended up with cuts calling for the attention of the campus nurse. So, the maintenance department put noticeable markers at eye level on frequently used glass doors.

As is true with the take-over of any new property, CSC had its share. One dormitory had no hot water in its bathrooms. Fortunately, in the warm fall days the men could temporarily hold their breath and adjust to taking cold showers. But only for so long. Patience was put to a test when it took days for maintenance to find the problem and make adjustments.

78

A more serious problem came during the unusual cold of the first winter. No storm windows had been built into any campus buildings. That was, obviously, a mistake for student dormitories. Students had trouble keeping warm. Placing a small portable electric heater didn't solve the problem. The electric overload on the circuits blew one fuse after another. Again, students needed to grit their teeth and tolerate the uncomfortable temperature through that first winter. Administration had the challenge of finding the money to pay for the installation of storm windows on all dormitories before the next winter.

Similar temperature problems occurred in the faculty homes. There the heating systems were located at one end of the building, creating serious problems for sending warmth to the bedrooms in the extreme opposite end. In subsequent years, when fuel costs began to skyrocket people had to accept the fact that heating costs in the Fort Wayne Scandinavian Village would always be higher than elsewhere.

Frequent Faculty Meetings

Faculty meetings were held almost weekly during the first two school years. Much time was spent dealing with administration. By at first letting the faculty participate in arriving at decisions, and in observing how administrators consulted whenever the faculty felt they should, mutual trust was built.

By January, 1959 the faculty had agreed on three basic committees, advisory in nature, handling administrative detail. The academic policies committee and the student life policies committee were also established.

North Central Accreditation also became an early concern. Dr. Paul Dressel from Michigan State University was employed as a consultant about this.

The faculty also decided that Graduate Record Examination Area and Aptitude Tests be administered to all seniors. This made it possible to compare performance of CSC students with students of major American universities. CSC students from the very beginning measured very favorably in these exams. Some of the CSC graduates, after many years, still point to the motivation and satisfaction which students derived from these comparisons.

79

Faculty members gave early attention to student dress in classrooms, dining hall, and chapel. Shirt and tie was the actual dress requirement. The story went around that all that was necessary to get an "A" in a certain religion class was to wear the proper shirt and jacket to that class.

Early attention was given to bringing in national authorities for convocations.

Daily devotions in the middle of the morning were held in the campus auditorium until the Kramer Chapel was built. Faculty members were in charge of the morning devotions. Church leaders occasionally were guest preachers. Students assisted with parts of the liturgy. Music under the guidance of Prof. Nuechterlein, organist and choir director, always provided a festive and worshipful atmosphere. Former students often mention the daily chapel as a major CSC contribution to their personal and spiritual development. Students conducted evening devotions in each dormitory lounge. Occasionally they would invite a faculty member to lead and then to socialize with them. Students also used the private dorm chapel rooms for personal devotions.

4. Campus Dedication

Dedication of the entire campus took place in a special service in the gymnasium on May 30, 1958. In addition to synodical officers and dignitaries, Eero Saarinen, the architect, also shared in dedicating the masterpiece he had created. He gets credit for bringing the majestic Scandinavian Village to Fort Wayne, Indiana.

B. A Decade of Rapid Growth. (1959-1969)

The sixties were definitely a decade of growth for Concordia Senior College. Growth showed itself professionally, financially, spiritually, and socially. By the end of the decade the school had reached its own distinctive identity in the religious community of LC—MS and in the higher education community of America.

1. Student Enrollment

The growth in student enrollment speaks for itself in the table below:

Year	Total Students
57-58	195
58-59	365
59-60	379
60-61	354
61-62	371
62-63	428
63-64	474
64-65	459
65-66	464
66- 67	503
67-68	514
68-69	492

Larger enrollments called for more faculty. The first year there were 21. The second year there were 30. By the end of the sixties the faculty numbered 48.

2. Growth in the Lutheran Church—Missouri Synod

There was a period of optimism and growth in the LC—MS as well. In 1958 a Synodical Survey Commission estimated an LC—MS membership of 4,311,400 by 1982. That meant that LC—MS would need a total of 13,687 pastors by that time. Subsequent history, of course, showed quite differently. Nevertheless, growth and optimism influenced all areas of the church and of CSC. For faculty and especially for administrators this provided the satisfaction of managing constant and steady growth. This also led to the expansion or CSC campus facilities such as the north classroom building and the east group of dormitories. Numerous off campus homes were also purchased to provide additional faculty housing. By June 30, 1968, 1822 graduates had received their B. A. degrees from CSC.

3. North Central Accreditation

A major event of this period was the full accreditation of Concordia Senior College by the North Central Association

81

(NCA) of Colleges and Universities. Three full years of faculty energy went into the preparation for the official visit by the NCA team. Accreditation simply had to be achieved. Some of the CSC opponents had strongly predicted that CSC would not be accredited. If CSC would fail now it would definitely become a laughing stock within LC—MS circles.

So, the engagement of Dr. Dressel as consultant and advisor, the careful organization of accreditation committees, the identification of items to examine, the identification of CSC strengths and weaknesses, the hours and hours of individual time and work necessary to do a careful job became a way of faculty life for three full years. Not only were the facts carefully identified, but the entire faculty, man to man, became familiar with them and was able enthusiastically to talk about them.

The NCA Report on Concordia Senior College supported everything said above.

"It would be difficult to imagine a college in which the institutional purpose is more clearly understood and universally accepted......The committee is convinced that this is an institution that knows what it is doing, and how, and why, and with what consequences.......Since it is less than five years old, its faculty has had more than the usual responsibility for educational planning. Few colleges know so much about themselves." (From the Report of an Accrediting Examination of Concordia Senior College, January, 1962.)

The formal accreditation of the college at the NCA meeting on March 29, 1962 came almost as an anticlimax. The CSC administration, the faculty, and the students understandably heaved a proud sigh of relief. Academically, CSC had come of age. The faculty dinner at Hall's in Fort Wayne, the enthusiastic celebration by President Neeb, by the faculty and their spouses is a highlight in the memory of all who participated.

Curriculum changes for the pre-ministerial students were relatively few during the decade of CSC growth. There were no changes in requirements in Philosophy, Hebrew, and Natural Science. Psychology requirements were changed from the original two required courses in Growth and Development to a third course in Abnormal Psychology. Addition of a three-week interim term provided the students and faculty opportunities to work in a variety of research areas and included off-campus travel-study courses.

4. Spiritual Growth

It was hardly possible to live on the CSC campus and not become spiritually stronger. Students who came here had a strong faith conviction. The faculty. likewise, was deeply faith motivated to provide an atmosphere and an education that would strengthen faith.

Everything that went on was centered on the Christian faith. The subjects which are taught are constantly related to the Christian faith. The attitude and example of faculty and staff influenced the students' spiritual life. The inter-student and the student-faculty relationship fostered it as well.

It is true that even in regular worship opportunities, the participation diminished as each year rolled on. It is also true that the life style of the world around them affected student attitudes and life style. Thus, the rebellious spirit of the sixties, also affected the attitude of CSC students. The same pressures influenced the attitude of the faculty and all who worked here.There was an ever increasing demand for change, for exerting one's self, of making one's own decisions rather than being guided by the systems of which we are a part.

But all in all, as time went on the campus influence was still strongly affected by the faith with which people came here and by the daily relationship to their God as they lived here.

5. Growth in Community Service and in Community Service

The social life which developed on the all male CSC campus was unique.

At the very beginning of each school year, incoming students had an opportunity to spend some social time in the home of one of the faculty members. Though these meetings were, to begin with, a bit awkward if not stiff, they soon moved into a growing sharing of common experiences and acquaintances. Before the evening was over, each student became better acquainted with the individuals who had come with him, and to remember the faculty member and his spouse as people who took a genuine personal interest in each student.

Usually there was an opening banquet for new students the night after the faculty home visit. This gave students an additional opportunity to experience the identity of faculty and spouses in a larger context and further to understand that the campus group enjoys fun.

Various social-cultural opportunities presented themselves as the year went on. Social-cultural dinners, spring banquets at the time the flowers were at their height on campus were a few highlights. The faculty follies occasionally brought the house down with faculty acting on stage, like "North by North Central" after the accreditation success. Students and non-academic staff and their families crowded the auditorium to get in on that fun.

The president each spring put on a major show in his back yard when food service outdid themselves to prepare special snacks and do it all up in style. To this the graduates would bring their parents and friends and faculty wives would help to make them experience a never to be forgotten affair. During the year the president would also put on special dinners for faculty only, like before school began in fall, after it ended in spring and at the annual spring faculty service recognition dinners.

The faculty ladies had their own special cultural groups. One was called the "culture vultures" where the ladies would gather to talk about books they had read. Another was led by Ella Wadewitz who taught the ladies some conversational German and occasionally invited them and their husbands to her home for parties.

In the area of service the faculty wives made the beginning. When a new faculty family moved into their home the faculty ladies would provide carry in meals until the newcomers were settled enough to do their own cooking. When a faculty wife was ill the other ladies again provided carry in meals for the family until the patient had recuperated enough to take over again.

Students, volunteered their services to many Fort Wayne and Allen County institutions. They also served many Lutheran congregations as Sunday School and Bible class teachers. A number of seniors took part time jobs as orderlies at Lutheran hospital.

Many patients commented favorably about CSC student visits and services.

A major service was the Red Cross Blood Bank. The Red Cross regularly parked its trailer on campus for a full day to enable students end faculty to come and make their blood donations. So generous was the participation that the local Red Cross chapter reported the outstanding CSC participation nationally.

The faculty met in the faculty lounge for a coffee break every school day morning after chapel. At the same time each morning the students gathered in the student commons for their little lunch and morning recess. These informal gatherings, completely voluntary, provided a good opportunity for socializing as well as provide easy personal contacts with colleagues.

Humor among faculty and students was common. The students had early given humorous identification to the dorm groups such as Harms' zoo, snob hill, quiet village (east lakers) and promised land. Faculty members, like Eric Malte and few others were known for their generous exchange of jokes. Curly Haas was the entertainer as he presented cartoons on campus events or certain campus individuals.

Spring pranks were received with mixed feelings by faculty and administrators. One that will be remembered brought all the classroom chairs outside and arranged them formally around the 10 acre lake. One year the entire first floor hallway of the administration building was filled with beer can collections which had been brought out of student collections in the dorms. Prank day usually disrupted class schedules and kept administrators from doing their normal job.

Another "prank" not too much appreciated by administrators and the maintenance department was the water fights between dormitories. Not only did this make extra work for maintenance but also called for unnecessary expenditures replacing fire extinguishers and water hoses.

All in all, however, the student-faculty spirit was good through the years.

6. The Arts

The college has an aesthetic impact upon anyone who tours the campus for the first time. It had the same impact when CSC students came the first time. Very subtly it continues to have that impact upon students and faculty and staff as they continue to live and work on campus day after day. There was always the impact of the dominant chapel, the circular relationship of the central building village, and the relationships which influenced those who moved in and out of their dormitories.

For this, of course, we need to thank Eero Saarinen who "wanted to create an environment appropriate to the intellectual and spiritual training of young men who would go on to professional studies in theology. There was the village concept, with the chapel placed in the center." The austerity which surrounded people who lived and worked here left a definite mark upon them when their contact with the campus came to an end. The campus itself is a majestic piece of art which one can find nowhere else but in the Scandinavian Village in Fort Wayne, Indiana.

Praise and adoration are also the theme of the pieces of art in the building interior. The "Te Deum" at the entrance to the library. The "Christ in Majesty" conveyed by the mosaic in the east end of the south classroom building. The hallway symbols in this building and those inside each class room silently keep repeating the reminder, this is God's place, and those who live here belong to God.

In addition to the visual experiences one receives, there is also the audio extravagance all around. The many choirs of powerful young male voices guided and directed by Dr. Herbert Nuecchterlein as well as the powerful sounds which only a young Joel Kuznick can daily create at the Schlicker organ to enhance peoples' worship and adoration.

Indeed, CSC belongs to God in the quiet Scandinavian Village north of the hustle and hurry on North Clinton Street and Coliseum Boulevard

Concordia Senior College Experiences Competition, Opposition, and Decline (1962-1975)

Glorious and majestic as it was, CSC in the Fort Wayne Scandinavian Village. could not last.. CSC was here to serve its purpose in God's glorious kingdom in its day. But it faced change as everything on earth has always done. It had come into existence by discussions and compromises. But the idea of a single separate upper level liberal arts college through which graduates of a synod wide system of junior colleges were required to go to enter the seminary in St. Louis was far from universally accepted.

A. Competition

The desire for B.A. degrees from synodically owned schools was quite universal among laity, teachers, pastors, and professors. But how to provide those bachelors' degrees was still a matter under discussion. While everyone had calmed down for a while to give the senior college a chance to get started, many people were far from satisfied that the "preferred" route into the LC-MS ministry was through the prep schools, senior college, and St. Louis Seminary.

Various questions were legitimately raised. If graduates of the Springfield Seminary are called to be LC-MS pastors in the same way as are St. Louis Seminary graduates then why is St. Louis the preferred route? In fact, why have Springfield at all? If Springfield needs to be changed to become equal, why not do it? While the Senior college in Fort Wayne was growing and succeeding, a man like George Beto, president of Springfield, was busy preparing Springfield for accreditation as St. Louis was.

Similar questions were raised about the two teachers colleges, Seward and River Forest. If pastors need a bachelor's degree from an accredited college then why not the teachers? And so the push for accreditation which was quite universally accepted drove each college and seminary of LC-MS to do their very best to move toward full accreditation as quickly as possible.

B. Competition-Opposition
1. St. Paul
a. Poehler

A very interesting parallel activity was that of St. Paul, Minnesota under the leadership of their presidents, Poehler, Stegemoeller, and Hyatt. Kenneth Kaden, in his centennial history of Concordia College, St. Paul, entitled "A Century of Service" gives the details from page 88 through 134.

"Pastor Poehler, a native Minnesotan and a 1924 alumnus of Concordia, had continued his close association with the college during his pastorates at three congregations in the state and envisioned the opportunities for increased service in the church." He was installed as president on September 15, 1946 Trinity Church in Minneapolis, where he had been pastor.

"The Synod's approval on March 18, 1947, of the senior college for pre-seminary students to complete their baccalaureate degree was met with great ambivalence on the Concordia campus...The faculty felt that this development was contrary to the direction American higher education was taking. President Poehler suggested that the synodical junior colleges in the most advantageous geographical and educational environment should be expanded into full four-year colleges with at least one major designed for pre-seminary liberal arts students." p. 91.

In February 1949 Poehler suggested that Concordia add a third year of college work. The program could eventually be enlarged to four years. The concept of expansion with coeducation was persistently presented to the church as one means of increasing Concordia's service to the Missouri Synod. BHE indicated that the supply of women teachers for LC-MS parochial schools was far from adequate. Concordia, St. Paul faculty prepared a two-year pre-education curriculum.

"Soon after he became president, Dr. Poehler, with the full support of the college Board, began the promotion of four-year liberal arts colleges with a core curriculum, common to both elementary education and pre-seminary programs. After Synod established the two year Senior College in Fort Wayne, St. Paul concentrated on expanding its offerings to a four-year teachers' college.

A 1959 San Francisco resolution to improve the quality of teaching in synod's elementary schools, renewed St. Paul's hope to establish the the third synodical teachers' college at St. Paul. The bachelor of arts program was carefully planned in consultation with accrediting agencies, presented to the 1962 Cleveland convention, approved, with enrollment in the senior college division limited to women.

In May, 1964 four liberal arts faculty members from the University of Minnesota validated Concordia's curriculum in the liberal arts. By 1967 Concordia College was granted full accreditation for its bachelor of arts program by the University of Minnesota.

By the closing session of the Detroit Convention in 1965, Concordia, St. Paul had become a four-year coeducational liberal arts college with an elementary education major. "The proverbial camel was almost halfway into the tent. Thoughts were already surfacing about other majors, especially those appropriate for pre-seminary students." p 106

"The years of Dr. W. A. Poehler's presidency were a period of notable change and growth......He provided Concordia with dynamic academic leadership that rarely accepted the status quo. 'Growth in Service' was not only a motto for his Concordia College, it was part of his ever changing vision for tomorrow. ...He assumed the leadership of an unaccredited six-year all-male school, and he left a fully-accredited coeducational four-year college whose goal was to provide professional and lay leadership for the church of today and tomorrow." p.114

b. Stegemoeller

Stegemoeller became Poehler's successor as the fourth President of Concordia. He had been on the faculty of Concordia Senior College in Fort Wayne under Dr. Neeb. In 1973 Synod had adopted a policy requiring that officers of LC-MS could not belong to Elim. Stegemoeller did. J. A. O. Preus wanted Stegemoeller to discontinue his Elim membership and got the local board to ask him to do so. Stegemoeller resigned instead. The reaction shook faculty, students and college supporters and divided them into two camps. Stegemoeller went on to lead the Minnesota private college association. Later he went to Columbus, Ohio to become president of Capital University.

Gerhardt W. Hyatt became Concordia, St. Paul's fifth president on Sept. 12, 1976. "An evaluation of Concordia's pre-seminary program in 1977 prompted the Board of Control to request approval by the BHE. Finally in December 1978, the BHE fully endorsed the pre-seminary curriculum of Concordia. The bachelor of arts program met entrance requirements for both seminaries of the Synod. With the closing of Concordia Senior College in Fort Wayne, Indiana, and the approval of Concordia's pre-seminary degree program in St. Paul, the camel was completely inside the tent of academic acceptability and respectability in ministerial education. The struggle had taken over 20 years."

So, while the Senior College in Fort Wayne prospered and grew, the opposition in St. Paul also prospered and grew and eventually replaced Fort Wayne's program.

2. Irvine

A similar way of competition and opposition grew elsewhere. Ironically, when Dr. Poehler retired from the presidency at St. Paul, he accepted a temporary assignment as acting president at Oakland, California. It was during that time that the decision to discontinue Oakland and instead to support the erection and development of a new college at Irvine, Calif. took place. Ironically, one of the author's colleagues at the senior college in Fort Wayne, with whom I was struggling to keep Concordia Senior College going in the 70's and beyond, predicted that Irvine had no reasonable chance to succeed and grow. Today, as one observes, it's interesting to note Concordia Senior College is gone and almost forgotten while St. Paul Minnesota and Irvine have grown by leaps and bounds.

3. Mequon

Another competitor and possible opponent of Concordia Senior College was Milwaukee. It was struggling to survive on an old, hemmed-in campus in the inner city of Milwaukee. It has since relocated to Mequon, which has grown into a major institution with successful extension programs at the Seminary in Fort Wayne.

Other colleges, like Bronxville, Seward, and River Forest were also powerful competition for Concordia Senior College.

C. Decline of Concordia Senior College

Without saying so, it is reasonable to assume that Dr. Neeb could see what was happening to the wonderful college which he had planned, designed and built into a pre-seminary liberal arts college with an upper level two-year program of outstanding recognition and performance. It was no longer accepted as the only preferred route into the LC-MS ministry. Years before, it had been decided at a convention in New York that Concordia Senior College graduates could also enroll at the Springfield seminary. Later, married students were allowed to enroll at CSC in Fort Wayne. Still later, girls were allowed to enroll at CSC and to graduate with a B.A degree just like the ministerial students.

A future planning committee worked with the faculty to expand the CSC offerings and to make majors available to areas other than pre-ministerial students. In other words CSC was led to fight for survival as a two-year upper level college competing with more and more other LC-MS colleges which were offering similar B.A. degree programs like Fort Wayne.

Early in this struggle Dr. Neeb reached retirement age. He retired and moved to St. Louis. He did some part-time teaching at Concordia Seminary.

Neeb's position was hard to fill. Dr. Bredemeier, former president of Fort Wayne Junior College, became that successor.

91

D. Summary of Concordia Senior College Decline

1. An upper level single separate liberal arts pre-seminary college in Fort Wayne, Indiana had been a long set of compromises from the very beginning.

2. Its competitors and opponents did not get their way, gave in to the majority to get something done, but kept on doing their own thing wherever they were:

a. Ann Arbor was promoted by many who had opposed selling the Junior College of Fort Wayne

b. People who wanted four-year colleges still did, in spite of CSC's success and excellence. Other junior colleges kept pushing for four years, introduced their own broader programs and moved toward eventual approval.

c. The whole idea of curriculum coordination with CSC taking the lead was never well received. Cooperation of junior colleges with CSC and the seminary with CSC did not fare well.

d. River Forest and Seward began introducing pre-ministerial programs on their own campuses.

e. The idea of a single preferred route, via St. Louis, was not well received by many clergy and laity.

3. CSC with its success and excellence was out of step with thinking of the masses and of the times in general

a. People more and more questioned the power and authority of institutions which grew out of tradition.

b. People, young and old, became more independent, wanted to make their own decisions, were reluctant to cooperate and especially to compromise with others.

c. The rebellious spirit of the sixties was at work at CSC among faculty and administrators as well as students. The spirit of the sixties had been at work in LC—MS generally, but trends for change were conservatively resisted, while opposition grew progressively.

4. Conservatives and Moderates were at work in their own way at their own places.

a. All the way from the adoption of the Brief Statement at the 1959 Synodical convention to the political victory for Jack Preus in 1969

b. "Gentlemen: it's a whole new ball game in Synod" said a prominent Fort Wayne layman after he returned from being delegate to the Denver convention

c. CSC, colleges and seminaries were drawn into the political Synodical action, in fact, in many instances may have been the sources and forces for much political action.

5. Changes and decline at CSC became a way of life in Synod:

a. The original spirit and drive were gone

b. Objectives and goals for ministerial training became less important

c. Competition, success, and survival tended to take their place

6. Regional competition in Synod grew

a. West Coast: Oakland closed, Portland hangs on, Irvine rises, and flourishes

b. Bronxville does its own thing

c. Milwaukee/Mequon grow and expand

d. Winfield is closed

e. Concordia, Missouri is changed into an academy

f. The Concordia University system is established

g. The two seminaries enroll students from wherever it can get them, with majorities not from syndical system schools. Ministry becomes a second career for a growing number of pastors. World wide mission opportunities call for special routes into church leadership.

The demand for change is all around us.

CHAPTER 11

Concordia Senior College Survival Struggle and End

A. Wide Attitude Changes

St. Louis seminary students in the nineteen-thirties used to delight in the peace which existed in the Missouri Synod. Somehow they had hoped that's the way ministry in the LC-MS would be.

They soon learned differently, however, when, for example as young pastors, they watched violent arguments in pastoral conferences, and especially as they experienced the political maneuverings which went on in their church. Their mail soon brought them unofficial publications which expressed opinions very different from those they'd been reading in the Lutheran Witness, or the Theological Monthly and the Walther League Messenger. Some of their former professors and the officers of Districts and of Synod, whom they had trusted and respected, were being severely criticized.

When "the forty-four" came out with their statement they were shocked to find that some well-known names were among those who questioned the direction in which Synod was going. Before long they found synodical conventions dealing with doctrinal problems among our own people and not just with the question whether or not we should work toward fellowship with other Lutherans. By 1959 the differences had become so strong that a synodical convention officially adopted "The Brief Statement" as a document to which all pastors should subscribe. However, a sizable number of pastors felt this added to the doctrinal positions to which they had sworn faithfulness, namely, the Scriptures and the Lutheran Confessions.

The division between the liberals and the conservatives became sharper as the years went on. People who wanted to change from the conservative positions which had controlled LC-MS for the first century of its existence became more and more vocal. Pastors in parishes as well as professors in colleges and seminaries become more and more divided.

When the rebellious sixties came along, the questioning of authority became a way of life. One could feel a change of attitude among students. Not only did this exist in classroom discussions but in their whole way of life. What one wanted for himself rather than what Christians needed to do in harmony dominated everyone's thinking. While Concordia Senior College did not experience riots like other campuses, students nevertheless questioned authority more than they had done before. The insistence on a systems route into the ministry via junior college, senior college, and St. Louis was challenged more and more. Not only students, but college presidents, faculties, and boards of control likewise questioned the need to cooperate with each other in the interest of Synod. More and more individual junior colleges with the backing of the regions in which they were located, moved farther and farther from the basic purpose of educating ministers and teachers into emphasizing general education.

Thus, the direction taken by Concordia, St. Paul, described in the previous chapter, also became a way of life in LC—MS: at Milwaukee, Ann Arbor, Bronxville, Winfield, and Irvine, CA. By the end of the sixties it seemed that everybody in LC-MS wanted their regional to become a four year school.

Naturally, this climate became a severe challenge to the "preferred route" which had been set up by synod in 1947. In fact, as synodical conventions dealt with subsequent problems, the "preferred route" became less and less "preferred." Concordia Senior College graduates could transfer to either synodical seminary, married students could enroll at CSC, and either seminary could enroll B.A. degreed students from any college, and girls could enroll at CSC as liberal arts students along with pre-ministerial students.

By the time the decade of the sixties was over, CSC was expanding its curriculum from pre-ministerial to general education. By 1973 the faculty was actually proposing that CSC be expanded into a four year college like other four year colleges which had arisen in synod.

B. The Political situation in LC—MS

By the 1969 Denver Convention the political battle had become a way of life. The extreme right actually took their cause to the sidewalks in front of the hotel in which the convention was held. Inside the hotel Prof. Martin Scharleman was asked to deal with what some considered to be liberal leanings which should not be tolerated in the LC-MS. So, Dr. Scharleman told the delegates that he was sorry for what had happened; and withdrew what he had written from further discussion.

Another surprising action at the Cleveland 1962 convention was the manner in which President Behnken dealt with one St. Louis Seminary graduate. The student had encountered various differences with some professors who were publicly teaching things that hadn't been taught that way before. He differed and disagreed to the the point where the faculty did not approve him for placement into the ministry of the LC-MS. The delegates were given to understand that he had taken the matter to public court, and was now personally appealing to the LC-MS convention to correct the matter for him. The convention did not solve the problem.

C. The Synodical Task Force Examines Ministerial Education in LC—MS

When Dr. Neeb retired from the presidency of CSC and moved to St. Louis, normal handbook procedures were followed to find a successor. A call went out for nominations, a CSC faculty committee studied the characteristics of each candidate, and reported their recommendations to the standard Synodical presidential election committee. Three names were presented. The election committee in executive session discussed them, and then requested more names. Later the faculty committee presented their recommendations. Eventually the election committee asked for a new list of candidates. This was done. The faculty committee again presented their choice. After a lengthy meeting the electors asked the faculty committee to include a candidate who was a current CSC faculty member. The committee included the name of H. G. Bredemeier, acting president. In a brief meeting the election committee reported that they had chosen Bredemeier to be the next president of CSC.

In this same synodical climate a task force was authorized by the 1973 Synodical convention to study the entire synodical ministerial education system and to report their recommendations to the Anaheim Convention in 1975.

The task force gave its report to the Anaheim convention. The report stated that the "Task Force is fully cognizant of the excellence of the preministerial education provided at Fort Wayne during the past 18 years." The task force also was aware of numerous requests for four year college status from junior colleges like Ann Arbor, Milwaukee and Irvine. It also emphasized that it "feels strongly that the traditional preministerial education must remain available to a significant number of our future pastors, and must include: 1) A curriculum directed specifically at pre-ministerial education. 2) A faculty pastorally trained, experienced, and committed to the preparation of men for the pastoral ministry, 3) An educational setting in which a large portion of the students are preparing for the pastoral ministry.

Then the Task Force recommended:

(1) That the Synod direct BHE to phase out Concordia Senior College, Fort Wayne...

(2) That a new upper level pre-ministerial curriculum be established on an existing campus,

(3) That it locate that preministerial program at Concordia, St. Paul, Minn. (This being a campus which had developed a four year education program, whose faculty was predominantly focused toward teacher education, and whose faculty had only a minority of pastorally trained and experienced faculty) and

(4) that BHE arrange to transfer the necessary faculty, library etc to St. Paul, MN

D. The Anaheim Convention

The 1975 Anaheim Convention floor committee presented Resolution 6-08A as follows:

"Whereas, In Resolution 6-07A we have established future direction for the synodical higher education system, therefore be it

1. Resolved, That the Board for Higher Education be directed to phase out Concordia Senior College at Fort Wayne as a separate educational institution:

a. that the pre-seminary program at Concordia Senior College, Fort Wayne, be relocated under the direction of the Board for Higher Education at Concordia Lutheran College, Ann Arbor, Mich, giving this college 4-year status;

b. that this phasing out and relocation under the direction of the Board for Higher Education be completed before Sept. 1, 1976;

c. that the present faculty and staff at Concordia Senior College, Fort Wayne, be given every possible consideration for placement as the pre-seminary program is relocated and staffed at Concordia Lutheran College, Ann Arbor, and as other positions are filled in the Synod; and

d. that the Board of Directors be authorized and directed to make necessary provision for funds to expedite the transfer; and be it further

2. Resolved, That the Board for Higher Education be directed to transfer Concordia Theological Seminary of Springfield, Ill., to the campus at Fort Wayne, Ind. by June 1, 1977, and be it further

3. Resolved, That the Board of Control of the Senior College be relieved of its duties and responsibilities after the transfer of property to Concordia Theological Seminary has been effected; and be it further

4. Resolved, That so much of the properties of the Springfield Seminary as are not required for synodical purposes be disposed of by the Board of Directors of the Synod and the proceeds therefrom be utilized in order to:

a. reimburse costs of relocation to and the capital improvements necessary on the Fort Wayne campus, and

b. the balance of funds, if any, be available to the Board for Higher Education for capital improvements of the system.

5. Resolved, That the Synod continue the development of Christ College Irvine according to previous convention resolutions...."

The convention consideration and action on this recommendation was postponed until near the end of the convention, when many of the delegates were thinking about hurrying action so they could go home. Fort Wayne delegates and their friends were given opportunity to speak, but the manner in which the discussion was handled, and the voices from Ann Arbor, and unofficial communications which took place soon showed that all attempted efforts to present reasonable points for consideration were useless and that the predetermined investigation, recommendation, and discussion would go.

The convention Adopted the above floor committee recommendations.

And so, the program of Concordia Senior College would come to an end. The program which it had established and developed would move to Ann Arbor, the resolution said, and make that school a four year college. And Concordia Theological Seminary would move out of their crowded campus in Springfield, Illinois and take over the prize-winning Scandinavian Village in Fort Wayne, Indiana. After that historical resolution the Anaheim convention recessed for lunch. Concordia Senior College faculty and friends gathered outside for a few words with each other, some understanding tears, and then made their way to the dining hall.

E. Concordia Senior College After the Anaheim Convention

The next day was the flight back home to Fort Wayne and to CSC. The author, as CSC Dean of Administration, wanted to get to the staff workers and speak to them about working with the CTS Administration during the time of the transfer of another institution to the Fort Wayne campus and during the last year or years of the CSC program.

A few days later the author made a trip to Springfield and assured Pres. Preus that he would do what he could to help implement the Anaheim resolution. His first concern was about CSC non-academic staff. He got the assurance that the Seminary was interested in taking the CSC staff on their payroll when they took over the Fort Wayne campus.

It was understood that CSC would maintain and operate the campus in Fort Wayne until it would be officially and legally transferred to CTS on June 30, 1977. At this meeting preliminary contacts were also made with Walter Campbell, CTS Business Manager and Howard Tepker, CTS Academic Dean to assure them that Edgar Walz as CSC Dean of Administration and H. G. Bredemeier as CSC President would be the official contact with CTS administrators until June 30, 1977.

It needed to be recognized by all that five different entities were involved in dealing with the "what," "who" and "when" questions in implementing the Anaheim Convention resolution. These five would include the administrators of Fort Wayne, Springfield, Ann Arbor, and Irvine with the BHE serving as consultant, advisor, and overseer.

1. Fort Wayne

Concordia Senior College went forward as close to normal as possible planning for and working with two classes of students who would be the last. Students cooperated beautifully with faculty and administration in dealing with the situation. Faculty, in addition to regular duties, needed to work on seeking positions after CSC was "phased out.' Surprisingly, the verbal promises given to Anaheim Convention delegates that the CSC program would be transferred to Ann Arbor were never carried. And only two of the 40 CSC faculty were eventually given positions on the Ann Arbor faculty. All others more or less were left to fend for themselves. So, Prof. Schramm, the CSC academic dean, took the additional responsibility of working with faculty with job hunting and referrals.

1975 through 1977 were anything but normal years for CSC faculty. Understandably, there was anger for what Synod had done. Frustration and helplessness were evident among faculty members, their spouses, and their families. In addition to their personal problems there was the contact with friends and relatives beyond the CSC campus and beyond Fort Wayne. Many

101

friends, relatives, and clergy were sympathetic and highly supportive. Some, however. were critical and suggested "naughty people simply got what they had coming." In the midst of it all, the faculty and their families did the best they could to conduct themselves in a loving Christian manner.

The graduation of the class of '76 was reasonably normal. The problem students needed to deal with was to decide what seminary to go to. Faculty and administrators, while sympathetic with their frustration, advised them to go the official route, to the remainder of St. Louis Concordia after the walkout. A few students decided to transfer to Springfield. Some students decided to attend Seminex in St. Louis whose former St. Louis seminary staff were in charge under President John Tietjen. (Later Synod dealt with the student frustration by giving Seminex graduates a chance for LC-MS clergy positions, after having gone through what one BHE staff member called the "dry cleaning" process.

F. The Year of Joint Occupancy

When H. G. Bredemeier and Edgar Walz drove to Springfield to discuss procedures for the move they were met by an unexpected surprise. They were told that BHE and Springfield had decided that the Seminary would move to Fort Wayne after July 1, 1976 not 1977 as they had assumed the Anaheim resolution meant.

This completely ignored the responsibility CSC had toward the junior class which was scheduled to enter CSC in Sept, 1975. Without communicating with CSC or consulting anyone at CSC BHE and Preus simply decided they would move to Fort Wayne after July 1, 1976. This, of course, meant that two schools would occupy and operate on the Ft. Wayne campus during 1976-1977.

Bredemeier and Walz were included in the discussion about a year of joint occupancy. Decisions had to be made about who would be responsible for what and where individual activities would take place. Basically, it was decided that CSC would be responsible for campus facilities and services operation until July 1, 1977. This meant that CTS would spend 12 months as tenants who would take over after a year and CSC would function like owner/operator landlord.

BHE sent Delphin Schultz to the CSC campus to study and determine who would work and function where during the joint year. Walz had already thought the matter through thoroughly. He told Schultz that library, chapel, dining hall, gymnasium, auditorium would be used jointly, with CSC being responsible for scheduling, maintenance and utility services.

The north classroom building would primarily schedule CTS classes and CTS administrative staff would have their offices in the second floor office spaces in the north classroom. Additional faculty office space for CTS would be provided in Dorm E and wherever other faculty offices would become vacant. The CTS president would occupy the president's home on campus and other CTS faculty who did not purchase their own homes would occupy vacant campus faculty homes as they became available.Book store and mail distribution would be operated by CSC and provide services for both institutions.

Schultz took these suggestions back to St. Louis. BHE wrote them up as the plan which BHE would direct CSC to follow during the joint year occupancy.

Frequent meetings between Walter Campbell, CTS business manager and Edgar Walz, CSC Dean of administration worked out further details about locations of staff and offices for business functions. Walz arranged for a separate room in the administration building to be available as the CTS business office on campus, taking care of payment of student fees and other finances and record keeping and accounting.

Movable property from CSC was to be divided among three different LC-MS educational institutions. CTS library directly connected with the former CSC curriculum would be sent to Ann Arbor. Some items of furniture and instructional equipment could perhaps be used at the new college which was under construction in Irvine. Springfield would bring items which they could use in Fort Wayne from Springfield. So representatives from various institutions spent considerable time on campus deciding what should stay, and what should be shipped to which institution. The interests of Springfield would be given preference for items to stay. The actual moves would occur after CSC

103

had closed its final independent year but before Springfield would move its belongings to Fort Wayne. CSC library items necessary for the last class would, of course, have to stay until the joint year was over.

Serving as CSC Dean of Administration during the joint year called for him to stand aside while decisions were made about what would come and what would go.

The writer protected the interests of CSC faculty and students and at the same time was as helpful as possible in assisting the other three institutions achieve their goals.

The biggest challenge came after July 1, 1976. Walter Campbell was in charge of loading and directing Springfield property moves and placement. Walz tried to help get them where they should go when they arrived in Fort Wayne.

Because of landlord- tenant interests, the placement of some items had to be placed into storage and wait for the final placement after July 1 of 1977, when Springfield would be completely in charge. Since the two institutions would share the chapel during the joint year, many of the Springfield chapel items were affected.

The Springfield chapel organ, however, was immediately installed in the campus auditorium, at the risk of encountering criticism from CSC individuals. The Springfield Luther statue was stored in "repose" in one of the empty campus faculty garages. After Springfield took over in 1977 the statue was moved to it's present location.

Considerable office furniture was immediately put to use in the north classroom building, where Springfield classrooms and administrative offices were located.

While immediate questions were raised by Pres. Preus about structural changes. His desire was to double faculty office dimensions in the faculty office building. He also wanted to change faculty homes to be more heat efficient and to provide air conditioning. It was agreed to wait with most of these alterations until the combined year was over and CSC faculty, staff and students would be gone.

The operation of two business offices, with two different accounting systems, and independent office employees became rather tricky. While Campbell spent most of his time with the

104

unsold campus in Springfield, Walz agreed to supervise detailed day to day business activities in Campbell's interest in Fort Wayne. A day or two of most of Campbell's weeks brought him to be in Fort Wayne, to approve and personally supervise as best he could under the circumstances.

During the year Walz and Campbell worked together with legal counsel to get things ready for the legal transfer by July 1, 1977.

Separate bank accounts, of course, were set up for the Seminary. The Seminary had its own budget under which to operate. It encountered new and unexpected costs with its operation in Fort Wayne. Fortunately, it could stay in the black during its final year of operation. CTS likewise handle its financial adjustments reasonably well.

As one would expect, a number of problems arose during the year. There was the difficulty with daily chapel worship. CTS believed that communion celebrations should be restricted to established congregations. CSC on the other hand had been been celebrating communion together with faculty, staff and students and their guests for years. So, the number of communions, by compromise was reduced. When communion was celebrated it was led by CSC faculty and CTS faculty were noticeably absent.

Preaching in chapel was handled by alternative scheduling of CTS and CSC faculty members. A few CSC faculty had difficulty restraining themselves from dealing with topics on which they knew there would be difference of opinion between Springfield and Fort Wayne. This led at least one Springfield faculty to bring a tape recorder to worship and gathering recordings of those CSC faculty he suspected as being troublesome.

Dining service menus and costs didn't present much of a problem. Communication about special meals for Springfield administrators and faculty did. This called for frequent reminders that all food service scheduling must, at least, be communicated via CSC administration offices.

Most of the conflicts were of a behind the scenes nature which could quietly be dealt with. Thanks to the faithful help of a student assistant, Ernie Savage, who understood the problems and was wonderfully skilled in working them out, we got through the year of joint occupancy.

105

While all the above joint events occurred, CSC faculty kept the college operating as normally as possible for the sake of the single senior class which was preparing to graduate. The faculty worked faithfully and as courageously as possible, under the circumstances. The students understood the difficulties under which we existed.

While all this happened, faculty and their families were preparing to end the wonderful time they had spent on the CSC campus. A event was the joint auction of faculty personal belongings, held in the gymnasium, in the form of a huge spring garage or moving sale.

CSC faculty socials were different insofar that considerable time was spent in encouraging each other, crying on each other's shoulders, and together sharing the anger under which all of us were struggling. One of the most frustrating experiences of the year was the last joint meeting with the CSC board of control. Periods of awkward silences marked the evening. Memorial plaques given by the board to recognize the services of faculty members, reluctantly accepted as graciously as possible, tucked away into faculty home drawers for as many years as it took each of us to adjust to the reality that CSC was at an end. Now those plaques hang more or less proudly in our offices as a thankful reminder of the "Camelot years" God had given us at Concordia Senior College.

When July 1, 1977 came it was a relatively simple matter to have a few remaining CSC professors remove their personal belongings from campus.

The exception was Bredemeier, Walz, and Walle. With BHE and CTS permission these three continued to use and work in Dorm A as their official offices. From these offices, a few CSC faculty continued to receive pay checks. This was also the place for administrative files which would later go to St. Louis. Walz employed a part-time secretary to help with correspondence, payroll, and financial records. This arrangement continued until Walz reached age 65. Thus, on June 30, 1979, the last CSC check was prepared and signed by Edgar Walz, Treasurer and H. G. Bredemeir, President, closing the Fort Wayne Concordia Senior College checking account and sending the balance to Arthur

106

Ahlschwede, Executive Secretary of BHE in St. Louis, MO. And that was, legally, the end of CSC.

In all legal records, Concordia Theological Seminary is the successor, owner, and responsible for former CSC matters.

Two CSC staff to this day continue their employment with CTS, Trudy Behning, Pres. Wenthe's secretary, and Mrs. Elwood, Dining hall employee. These two carry memories of historical Scandinavian Village events quietly, and make them available when asked, and when appropriate.

CHAPTER 12

Concordia Theological Seminary Occupies the Scandinavian Village

Concordia Theological Seminary has replaced Concordia Senior College in Fort Wayne, Indiana. The Scandinavian Village is still there. It's a quiet place hidden behind the woods off north Clinton Street . As we go back there now we look for changes.

A. Campus Changes-Buildings and Grounds
1. Grounds Changes (See Campus Map on following page)

The most obvious change is the entrance sign. (See photo) From the temporary sign at CSC ground breaking, to the temporary combination during the year of joint senior college and seminary occupancy in 1976, all the way to the present marker which simply reads: CONCORDIA THEOLOGICAL SEMINARY. Many Fort Wayne people didn't really understand the change. Some still call it the college. Others speak of Concordia Senior College faculty as retirees of the seminary.

The road still winds its way up the hill. But the creek with its white stone banks catches our eye more readily than ever. A rustic foot bridge leading into Concordia's deer country, gives one a feeling of mystery.

As we ascend up the hill our eye is caught by the huge statue of young Luther standing firmly on the edge of the wide open campus looking back to the crowded inner part of Springfield, Illinois whence he came. The statue clearly identifies the Scandinavian Village as a Lutheran territory.

Campus Map

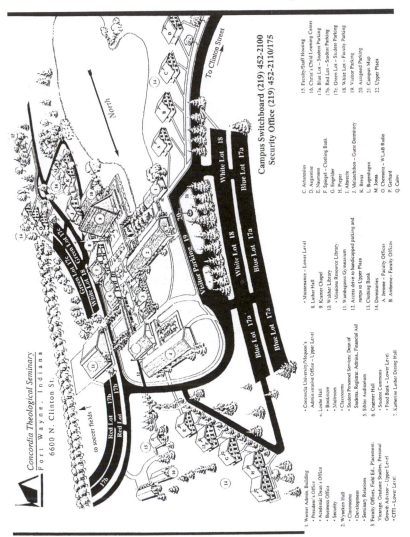

Concordia Theological Seminary
Fort Wayne, Indiana
6600 N. Clinton St.

North

To Clinton Street

Campus Switchboard (219) 452-2100
Security Office (219) 452-2110/175

1. Werner Admin. Building
   • President's Office
   • Academic Dean's Office
   • Business Office
   • Security
2. Wyneken Hall
   • Classrooms
   • Development
   • Seminary Relations
3. Faculty Offices, Field Ed., Placement,
   Vicarage, Graduate Studies, Personal
   Growth Advisor – Upper Level
   • CITI – Lower Level

• Concordia University/Mequon's
   Administrative Office – Upper Level
4. Loehe Hall
   • Bookstore
   • Mailroom
   • Classrooms
   • Student Personnel Services; Dean of
   Students, Registrar, Admiss., Financial Aid
5. Sihler Auditorium
6. Cramer Hall
   • Student Commons
   • Food Bank – Lower Level
7. Katherine Luther Dining Hall

• Maintenance – Lower Level
8. Luther Hall
9. Kramer Chapel
10. Walther Library
   • Missions Resource Library
11. Wambsganss Gymnasium
12. Access drive to handicapped parking and
   ramps to Upper Plaza
13. Clothing Bank
14. Dormitories
   A. Jerome – Faculty Offices
   B. Ambrose – Faculty Offices

C. Athanasius
D. Augustine
E. Naumann
F. Spiegel – Clothing Bank
G. Engelder
H. Pieper
I. Albrecht
J. Melanchthon – Guest Dormitory
K. Brenz
L. Bugenhagen
M. Jonas
O. Chemnitz – WLAB Radio
P. Gerhard
Q. Calov

15. Faculty/Staff Housing
16. Christ's Child Learning Center
17a. Blue Lot – Student Parking
17b. Red Lot – Student Parking
17c. Green Lot – Student Parking
18. White Lot – Faculty Parking
19. Visitor Parking
20. Assigned Parking
21. Campus Map
22. Upper Plaza

The spacious well-kept lawns still blanket the rolling hills of the former Kramer farm. Many of the towering trees which once shaded the sidewalk from the dorms to the campus center have been removed. A speed bump slows the traffic at the parking lot curve. Parking lots are identified with colored markers to indicate where faculty and staff and students, as well as visitors and disabled may park. Visitors can get some idea of streets and building locations from the map posted on the board near the administration buildings.

Strange names on campus buildings confuse the old time visitor who still prefers to call the dorms by their simple original Saarinen alphabetical labels. The "Wambsganss" name on the gymnasium is meant to remind the baseball historians of the unassisted triple play made by that Fort Wayne Lutheran pastor's son.

Three more exterior campus changes should be pointed out to the old time visitor. The small bell tower at the east end of the chapel holds the bell brought from Springfield. This is happily tolled by each fourth-year student on the day he completes his last requirement for graduation from Concordia Theological Seminary. The upper plaza has been completely changed from the original blacktop pavement to an ornamental garden area with artistic tiles, designs and water pools. As one descends to the lower plaza one walks past a waterfall which on windy days sprinkles whoever goes by. The ornamental white rocks on its shore highlight the beautiful lake.

2. Building Changes

Concordia Theological Seminary has made many building changes in the Scandinavian Village. These include: (1) A glass enclosed entry way into Kramer Chapel, (2) a public address sound system in the chapel. (3) The former health center converted into an beautifully furnished lounge. This meeting room is used for special gatherings of faculty, visiting groups and for social gatherings. (4) The dining hall has rebuilt its serving system to provide an efficient cafeteria. (5) The student commons provides a snack service and recreation equipment, a large television, and class photos of graduates during the years that CTS operated in Fort Wayne. (6) Faculty offices in the building

111

between the classroom buildings have been enlarged to double their original size. (7) A complete print shop has been added on the lower space under the auditorium. (8) Faculty and student association offices are located in the two classroom buildings. (9) The former speech area in the south classroom building has been remodeled into administrative offices . (10) Former dorm "A," now labeled as "Jerome" houses faculty offices. In the lounge of Jerome, stands the former Concordia Junior College faculty room table dating back to the early part of the twentieth century. It is surrounded by very comfortable modern swivel chairs and provides space for faculty and campus committee meetings. (11) Dorm"B" is currently being converted into additional offices. (12) A few dormitories are used for housing single students. (13) Most former dormitories have been converted to other uses, such as food bank, clothing bank, nurseries for faculty children. (14) Dorm "O" is used by the Fort Wayne Lutheran radio station. (15) A number of dormitories are being developed for seminary retreats and for other rental purposes.

All the faculty homes have been extensively remodeled. The former sliding doors to the patios have been replaced with more temperature efficient openings. All homes have been air conditioned. Their original uniform exterior gray has been replaced with a variety of four or five colors. This gives the area a residential community instead of a barracks appearance. An extension built on the east side of the president's home provides ample space for social gatherings.

B. Activity Changes -
The People who Live and Work There
1. Administration

Dr. Robert Preus, president of CTS and his brother J.A.O.Preus, who was then president of Synod, the synodical task force, and other synodical schools terminated CSC in Fort Wayne and replaced the Scandinavian Village with CTS.

The two Preus theologians and educators were also skilled political leaders. That skill was evident from the very beginning of Robert's Fort Wayne administration. He left the day to day educational concerns to other administrators who worked under him, while he devoted a major proportion of his time was to doctrinal and leadership matters beyond the educational concerns of the seminary. During the summers, for example, he spent most of his time at his lake property in Minnesota where regular telephone contact with his secretary kept him informed about what went on in Fort Wayne.

During the school year, Dr. Preus taught courses in Systematics, his area of expertise. During his administration he initiated the systematics convocations which are still a major annual campus activity.

Considerable resistance arose when the Board of Regents "Honorably" retired Dr. Preus from the seminary presidency at the age when LC-MS presidents normally handed over their responsibilities to a new administrator. That board decision led to a number successive interim presidents.

Through these years the author, who was closely involved with CTS activities as an adjunct part-time professor, observed numerous changes in top CTS administrative positions. This included all areas of seminary activities, such as deans of students, academic deans, business administrators, registrars, financial aid officers, department heads and others.

2. Faculty

The decision to move Concordia Theological Seminary from Springfield to Fort Wayne was predominantly an administrative decision. The faculty was not consulted about moving. Some of the old time CTS faculty did not like the idea of giving up their homes and friends in Springfield and moving to Fort Wayne. Others of the faculty wanted to remain in Springfield but were strongly urged to come along with the move. Others, for the sake of the seminary felt they must give up their Springfield connections and move to Fort Wayne. None of the them were strongly welcomed by the Fort Wayne community, by the majority of the Fort Wayne Lutheran clergy or laity, and not by the remaining former CSC faculty and staff.

The writer had accepted the move as an official decision of the church of which he had been a lifetime member and a long time Fort Wayne pastor/professor. So, he did what he could as

CSC Dean of Administration to help CTS faculty and administration complete the move and to help them get established in these new surroundings. A number of CTS faculty made it a point personally to share their concern about what had happened to CSC administration, faculty, and staff. One CTS administrator indicated how much they needed the services which only the author could provide both administratively and academically.

The community, generally, did not reach out with open arms to welcome the new professional educators and their families.

Today the present administration is making a noticeable effort to improve these relationships.

It must be emphasized that the CTS faculty and staff are conscientious and capable in their areas of activity. The CTS faculty are capable scholars and teachers in their areas just like the CSC faculty had been in their areas of expertise. A noticeable difference, however, is the greater amount of writing and publication of books and magazine articles. For the seminary faculty, writing and publishing in their area of expertise is a regular way of life while, with CSC, it was more the exception. The same is true about the extent to which CTS faculty participates in denominational committees and leadership positions. On week ends many CTS faculty travel to distant parts of the country, yes of the world, to speak, to deliver lectures, to conduct seminars, or to preach.

Because of frequent professorial absences, much of the academic detail is placed into the hands of faculty and administrative secretaries.

3. Staff

Besides secretaries, food service workers and maintenance workers, staff at the the seminary includes many professional people. There are writers, editors, fund raisers, financial office workers, and educational staff. In addition, staff also includes a sizable number of ordained clergy who work in areas like the library, recruitment, development and other positions.

This raises some questions, and even little problems, when it comes to social campus functions. Sometimes there are staff meetings of secretaries, food service, maintenance and others, which are not of primary importance to clergy staff. At other

114

times there are faculty and their family gatherings which are of interest also to ordained staff and their families.

4. Board of Regents

The Boards of control for synodical educational institutions are normally elected from pastors, teachers, and lay members within the general region in which the school is located. For seminaries, and teachers colleges as well as the senior college that was not the case. So, their boards of control were elected from pastors, teachers, and lay members who came from various wide geographical areas of Synod.

With the more open political interests in Synod over the last three decades, or so, political characteristics and representations have become much more obvious in selecting boards of regents for seminaries, teachers' colleges, and liberal arts colleges. Over these decades the voting lists which have been prepared for and distributed to convention delegates have directed voters to choose people of certain political characteristics rather than educational and theological concerns. As a result there have been members on boards of regents who were not especially knowledgeable about educational concerns. As a result, a number of synodical institutions have received comments, if not notations, about the absence of certain standard educational factors and procedures at their institutions.

In many instances the political interests expect boards of regents to make decisions which rightfully should be made by faculties and administrators. The problem is similar to that in congregations that have grown from the time when votes' assemblies decided details about how to paint a wall, what kind of paint to use, and what color to make them. The larger an organization becomes the more necessary it becomes to have routine detail taken care of by people who are closest to the day to day activities.

Boards of control have the responsibility of dealing with LC-MS's doctrinal and educational purposes of an institution while the people who are engaged to run the institution must have the trusted authority to accept those purposes and who have the professional knowledge and skill to do that efficiently. Just as little as one would expect a board of regents to know how to teach the

115

details of public speaking, just so little should the board be expected to make detailed decisions which are the duty of individual faculty members or administrators.

The ideal relationship, of course, is the one where board members clearly understand their educational rights and duties, and where faculty and administrators know theirs. In such a relationship everyone respects the limits of functions and duties, and gives support and strength to individuals faithfully and joyfully to do what God expects them to do.

5. Seminary Students

Most seminary students today are second career men. A fairly common route is to become LC-MS teachers and then to decide to go to a seminary and become a pastor.

Most second career ministerial students are in their thirties and forties and some even in their fifties by the time they enter the seminary. So, most of them have been away from academic situations for some time. That makes many of them apprehensive about classroom routines, and even to wonder whether they can make the grade or not.

On the other hand, there is a minority of students who have the advantage of moving on to a higher level of studies. They're still in the swing of academic activities. Older and more experienced students also have the advantage of greater depth in their learning and often are more highly motivated.

In addition, most second career students are married. As such they're required to accept various roles in their student life. Many of them need to be student and spouse and parent and often part-time wage earner. The advantage of these multiple roles is early preparation for the multiple roles of parish ministry. Sometimes, however, the demands become excessive and depressing.

The students' financial situation is another important factor one needs to recognize. There is a limited number of second career students who have been very successful in their former careers. Some, like military retirees may, indeed, come with a sizable pension income. Most of them, however, need to make adjustments to a lower income than they've had before they came. In a few cases, when emergency expenses confront them

116

they need to go deeply into debt or even adjust to more than a four year period of time to complete their seminary courses,

Students at Concordia Theological Seminary are very different from what students at Concordia Senior College had been. The Fort Wayne community and the Lutheran churches in the city and surrounding counties have adjusted to the changes and are more and more ready to accept the realities and to feel happy and proud of "their seminary."

6. Seminary Visitors, Friends, and Patrons

Over the years people who come to a Concordia Campus in Fort Wayne have changed significantly.

Concordia College, the Maumee Avenue predecessor of the Senior college had built up a loyal support group throughout Indiana, Ohio, and Michigan. Pastors were happy and proud to be alumni of that college. Congregations who had sent their sons also had built commodity support systems. Farm produce and cash donations, however, stopped when the old college was sold and the Senior College moved in.

The neighboring Michigan Lutherans most noticeably went to work to establish their own Concordia at Ann Arbor, Michigan. Lutherans who used to participate in junior college functions, tended to shift their loyalties to Fort Wayne Concordia Lutheran High School.

Concordia Senior College needed to establish a support system of its own. Over time the crowds that came to campus for special occasions, especially musical functions, were attracted by Schlicker Organ and Concordia Senior College chorus presentations. Before too long the chapel was filled by Fort Wayne Lutherans and other church friends. Catholic clergy and sisters were in regular appearance at all of the campus functions. Over time, more and more members of the Lutheran churches of the cities and neighboring counties also participated.

A noticeable change of visitors to the Scandinavian Village has occurred in the last twenty years. When the Seminary first became responsible for their own public functions, a number of Fort Wayne Lutherans, who were never close to Concordia Senior College came just to be loyal to the new institution.

117

Over time a sizable number of Lutherans from small town congregations of Indiana and neighboring states regularly appeared. As the president of the Indiana District brought in more and more pastors who were graduates of Springfield to fill pastoral vacancies, they, of course, naturally went out of their way to support their alma mater. Over time the Indiana District has brought a predominance of Fort Wayne Seminary graduates into many small town churches, to the rural areas of Adams Country, and as assistant or associate pastors in Fort Wayne Lutheran churches. Now, of course, the Fort Wayne graduates are self-evidently proud of the school from which they graduated and do everything they can personally and through their members to be faithful to the LC-MS seminary in Fort Wayne.

Dr. Dean Wenthe, who in 1996 took over the leadership of the Seminary as president, is making a very strong and hopefully successful effort to win increasing local Lutheran and community support to Concordia Theological Seminary. Over time, and hopefully soon, a growing new element of supporters will be coming to the Fort Wayne Scandinavian Village.

CHAPTER 13

Concordia Theological Seminary Lives on in the Scandinavian Village

A. Campus Purpose

Activities in the Scandinavian Village of Fort Wayne, Indiana have always been involved with preparing pastors for the Lutheran Church—Missouri Synod. That was the purpose for the campus which the 1953 LC-MS convention authorized. That was the purpose for CSC which provided the two upper college years to ministerial students before they entered a synodical seminary from 1957 to 1977. And that is the purpose for which the 1975 LC—MS convention authorized the Springfield Seminary to take over the Scandinavian Village.

That has been the purpose of LC-MS's ministerial training system for more than 150 years . St. Louis from its beginning placed more emphasis on the study of theology while the seminary which started in Fort Wayne was more concerned about getting men ready to take over congregations' pastoral duties as quickly as possible. So, from the beginning, the St. Louis seminary became known as the theoretical seminary and the Fort Wayne (Springfield) seminary as the practical seminary. Graduates of both seminaries were accepted as fully qualified for pastoral ministry in LC-MS.

Subconsciously, however, the St. Louis seminary was thought of as THE seminary. Over time, however, the difference between the two schools became less and less. A study of Greek and Hebrew was required of all St. Louis students. These languages were offered at the Springfield seminary on an optional basis until the 1950's or '60's . Since the 1970's, entrance and graduation requirements of the two seminaries are almost identical.

As pastoral responsibilities in congregations in America placed a growing emphasis on people relations tasks, such as counseling, pastors from both seminaries have been prepared with those skills. Administrative skills related to the needs and

119

cultural situations of specific congregations have also become more important.

CTS has been aware of these changes. While there is always a hesitance to change, the realities of pastoral candidates' desires and of calling congregational requirements have, over time led to major curricular changes. Thus, one can usually expect an ongoing tension between the practical and the theological (theoretical) dimensions of a seminary curriculum. Faculty will normally push the importance of their own specialty.That tension has existed and continues at CTS in Fort Wayne.

Another notable educational emphasis at CTS during its years in Fort Wayne has been missions. CTS brought an interest in and some provision for working with Spanish and black students when they moved to Fort Wayne. Soon after their move CTS called a long-time missionary leader from Africa to become an important part of its faculty and to become the head of its missions department.

Over the years the missions department has grown rapidly. Not only have ministerial students been exposed to courses in missions, but an accredited Doctor of Missions program has been established. Students for the Doctor of Missions degree have been recruited from American parishes as well as from various foreign mission fields.

A recent emphasis on missions has been set up for several Russian students and their families. Subsidized by a million dollar restricted gift from an interested individual, these Russians have spent an academic year on campus. Through an interpreter they have studied theology with the hope that they can take a leadership role in establishing a Lutheran seminary in Russia.

The mission emphasis has also alerted the seminary to intercultural concerns. Understanding cultural backgrounds has been established as a basic preliminary requirement of missionaries and their spouses as well as the development of language skills. This intercultural emphasis has also led to a need for understanding differences from the traditional Lutheran cultural lifestyles in America.

As a result of these recent cultural emphases understandable tensions have arisen between academic departments and have reached out to numerous congregations and pastors in LC-MS. As the church works through these tensions various changes in theological education are likely to result. Bringing the changeless Christ to an ever changing world has once again become a major challenge to CTS.

B. Campus Activities

The day to day activities on campus are driven by the seminary's basic purpose. That focuses attention upon what goes on in the classroom. Here the Gospel message of the Old and New Testament, the organization of Bible doctrines with an understanding of the historical context within which they exist, and the development of skills of communication, including understanding the people and their culture are all emphasized.

The annual academic calender extends through all months of the calendar year except August.

Recruitment activities under the administration of recruitment officers are ongoing. The pastors and missionaries of LC-MS likewise are are a part of the recruitment system as they model and personally encourage individuals who may be interested in studying for the ministry. This, in recent years, has shifted extensively to older men, many of whom decide to make a vocational shift and go into the study for the ministry as a second career. That, in turn, introduces an ever increasing shift to activities involving child care, elementary and secondary education for students' children, and part to full time employment for spouses, and part-time jobs for men. Thus, a whole system of special provisions like food bank, clothing bank, and child care center as well as special activities for student spouses are common on campus.

Financial management to support academic and other activities are an essential part of operating CTS. The vice president for business affairs and his staff, take care of this. The development officers and staff and the seminary president are extensively involved with soliciting donors. This is in addition to the subsidy that is available from the LC-MS. There is also a growing need to help support students and in some cases their families who come from foreign countries. All of this presents an enormous challenge to develop new sources of funds for current operations and also to increase endowments to support student aid.

Good stewardship requires the development of building and facilities uses beyond ministerial education requirements. As a result, facilities are rented to The Concordia University of Mequon, Wisconsin, for classroom and office space. Since most of those college classes are in the evening, they can be readily scheduled in addition to seminary daytime classroom needs. The evening classes, however, call for building management and operation people to be, likewise, scheduled during the evening hours.

One entire dormitory is rented to the Indiana District Lutheran FM radio station. Dorm O provides that group with space for staff and technical equipment.

In addition, a number of other group activities of businesses and educational institutions are provided, especially during the summer months.

The spacious campus, with its athletic fields is extensively used by Lutheran elementary schools Thus, one can expect to find people of all ages, in addition to regular campus visitors, and students and staff to move around on campus almost constantly.

The present administration is very active in bringing more and more people to campus for seminars and retreats. .

As time goes on, greater and greater use of the Scandinavian Village in Fort Wayne is to be expected.

Conclusion

We have looked at the detail of training men for ministry in the Lutheran Church-Missouri Synod. Beginning with the simple Log Cabin in Perry County, Missouri, to the red brick building which stood tall through the years in south St. Louis on to the majestic ninety acre cloistered campus in suburban Clayton, Missouri. From the humble beginnings in Wyneken's and Siehler's parsonage in Fort Wayne to the three-story red brick building which for more than a century housed men while preparing to be pastors and teachers. From the twenty acre campus on Maumee Avenue to the spacious two hundred acre Scandinavian Village. From the "practical" seminary later moved to St. Louis in exchange for the Junior college "prep" school, then on to Springfield and eventually back to Fort Wayne. From the twenty year bridge known as Concordia Senior College which led from a German "gymnasium" through seminary route to the more American way of making pastors by accepting B. A. degreed men from church or secular colleges and preparing men for pastoral calls in a standard four-year seminary curriculum.

Through it all an ongoing emphasis of the basis of God's Word in the Old and New Testament and of the Lutheran Confessions as the theological foundation. All this to equip pastors to bring the Gospel of Jesus Christ to save sinners for everlasting life with God in heaven. Two majestic campuses stand there at 801 De Mun in St. Louis and 6600 N. Clinton in Fort Wayne waiting for men to come and prepare to carry out Christ's command to "go and make disciples of all nations."

And as we think about it we are reminded of hundreds, yea, thousands of professors and administrators of the ministerial training systems who have given their lives of service to operate LC-MS's schools of the prophets through the years. Behind them stood spouses and families faithfully supporting them and urging them to face the challenges and frequent hardships that confronted them. Many of their dreams and disappointments are forgotten as we focus upon bricks and stones and mortar as symbolic reminders of what God has done through them.

So it is especially with the Scandinavian Village in Fort Wayne. It took so long in coming, it performed so proudly for twenty short years, and now it stands there as a memory and bridge while others follow on. People come and do their thing and move on while the institutions they served live after them.

And so it shall ever be as we follow Christ's directive of: "Go ye into all the world, and preach the Gospel to every creature." And as we go we keep on trusting

His comforting assurance: "Lo, I am with you alway, even unto the end of the world."

And so we pray:

"Swift to its close ebbs out life's little day;
Earth's joys grow dim, its glories pass away;
Change and decay in all around I see.
O Thou, who changest not, abide with me!" TLH 552, 2.

Bibliography

BOOKS:

Bredemeier, Herbert G., Concordia College 1839-1957. Fort Wayne, In., 1978.

Dau, W. H. T., Ebenezer. St. Louis, Concordia Publishing House, 1922.

Heintzen, Erich H., Prairie School of the Prophets, St. Louis, Concordia Publishing House, 1989

Kaden, Kenneth P., A Century of Service. St. Paul, Minn., 1993.

Polack, W. G., The Story of C. F. W. Walther. St. Louis, Concordia Publishing House, 1935.

Proceedings of LC-MS Convention, Fort Wayne, 1923.

Proceedings of LC-MS Convention, St. Louis, 1926

Proceedings of LC-MS Convention, River Forest, 1929

Proceedings of LC-MS Convention, Milwaukee, 1932

Proceedings of LC-MS Convention, Saginaw, 1944.

Proceedings of LC-MS Convention, Chicago, 1947.

Proceedings of LC-MS Convention, Milwaukee, 1950.

Proceedings of LC-MS Convention, Houston, 1953.

Proceedings of LC-MS Convention, St. Paul, 1956.

Proceedings of LC-MS Convention, New York, 1957.

Proceedings of LC-MS Convention, Denver, 1969.

Proceedings of LC-MS Convention, New Orleans, 1973.

Proceedings of LC-MS Convention, Anaheim, 1975.

Walle, Oscar T., Lest We Forget-A History of Concordia Senior College 1957-1977.

Springfield, IL., 1978.

137

PERIODICALS:

Lutheran Witness 1947-1975

Progressive Architecture, December, 1958

Spire, Concordia Senior College, Vol. 1. 1959

VIDEO:

Concordia Theological Seminary, "Campus, Artwork, History" 1986

DATE DUE